Runaway

Notes on the Myths that Made Me

ERIN KEANE

Belt Publishing

Printed in the United States of America
First edition 2022
1 2 3 4 5 6 7 8 9

ISBN: 9781953368317

Belt Publishing
5322 Fleet Avenue
Cleveland, Ohio 44105
www.beltpublishing.com

Cover art by David Wilson
Book design by Meredith Pangrace

Author's Note:
This is a work of nonfiction. Some names have been changed and are so noted
in the text. Some personal details have also been obscured to protect privacy.
Conversations, scenes, and situations have been recreated and dramatized using the
best recollection of interview subjects, and supported, when possible, with media
accounts, public information, and other research.

For my mother and my brother,
and for Megan and Alexis.

CONTENTS

1
She's a Bright Girl

Of all the lies I once believed about my mother and father, the biggest was the one I told myself. For most of my life, I reveled in my origin story as a daughter of the grittier, downtown version of Woody Allen's *Manhattan*, a movie I loved fiercely, perhaps because it too demanded a certain amount of self-deception. In 1972, my mother was fifteen years old—a beautiful runaway from a respected military family, living as an adult under a fake name in New York's East Village—when she met my father at Googie's, her favorite bar. They fell in love and married that year. He was a recovering heroin addict, sporadically employed and with a criminal past, a self-taught, bullshitting Renaissance man who drove a cab and wooed her with barstool poems. He was also the same age as her father.

Googie's is where I thought my family's story started, when he was thirty-six and nobody knew—or more likely, nobody cared—that my mother was a child, claiming to be in her twenties with a name and a backstory that had nothing to do with being the daughter of an Army officer and a mother in bespoke beaded dresses who saw cotillion and college in her daughter's future, not hitchhiking across the country, sleeping in subway stations, hanging around bars with penniless actors and artists, drinking for cheap. After all, in *Manhattan*, we don't see what seventeen-year-old Tracy was doing before she starts dating Isaac, the twice-divorced protagonist who is her father's age and who cracks self-conscious jokes about it in front of his friends. We're not actually supposed to care. A girl becomes visible to the world, stories like *Manhattan* taught me, when a man appears next to her in the frame.

It is embarrassing now to admit how much I believed in *Manhattan* and for how long it remained one of my favorite films. And yet I know I'm not alone. A movie doesn't become a perennial best-of without a certain cultural consensus behind it. (See the 2007 critical outcry from *New York* magazine after the "doddering" American Film Institute dropped *Manhattan* from their Best 100 Films list. The magazine protested that the movie is "an absolutely perfect film, one of the few that, a hundred, two hundred years from now, they'll still be watching, list or not." Call me impressionable, but 2007 was the year I started my own career as a culture writer, and I gave a lot of weight to what *New York*'s critics wrote.) That same consensus has long positioned men's narratives as the world's de facto serious stories, even when the fictions they contained were wildly self-indulgent. After Allen's adopted daughter Dylan refused to stay silent as an adult about her allegations that he molested her when she was a child, the cultural consensus now about Woody Allen is, to quote actor Wallace Shawn's defense of him, that he is a "pariah." As a supporter of survivors of abuse and exploitation, I have no appetite for his work anymore. But I can't pretend I never did. If you had asked me ten years ago if I thought there was anything wrong with the relationship Allen wrote for his stand-in Isaac and the teenaged Tracy, a role that garnered Mariel Hemingway an Academy Award nomination, I would have waved away the question with a noncommittal shrug. To make great art, we must create space and empathy for characters who make bad choices, right? And that grace we extend to fiction has long bled over to include the art's makers and their misdeeds.

At long last, that's beginning to change. Prominent men in numerous industries have been exposed, denounced, and diminished over their exploitations of power, including with teenage girls. Headlines treat those men as powerful outliers. But I don't believe they're special. Their choices were formed by a culture that romanticizes men who have big appetites that shape their allure and cause their downfall, all while casting aside the unruly girls left in their wake as damaged goods.

I am also of that culture, a product shaped by it. My father, the complicated seeker; my mother, his beautiful life raft. I never questioned their marriage's power imbalance, how it tilted everything in his favor. He died when I was five, which transformed him into a romantic figure in absentia—a fantasy, a celebrity of sorts, intimately knowable and shrouded in mystery all at once. My mother outlived him, moved on from his death, and built a new life for herself and us. But I remained loyal to him in the most childlike way, nurturing the hole his absence left in me, tending its jagged borders as a memorial to his tragic ruin. Flawed male protagonists and their dissolute creators, self-destructing musicians with sordid reputations—I welcomed them into that space. I craved their voices because I couldn't hear his.

On their first date, my father took my mother to a seafood restaurant on Sixth Avenue in Greenwich Village that I think must have been the original Captain's Table. Red, as he was called because of his ginger hair and beard, was tall, barrel chested, and blue eyed. As he steered her toward their table, he leaned over to murmur in her ear, "Mafioso hang out here." My mother believed him. He had a way of saying things that made them sound true. She had wide green eyes, high cheekbones, fair skin, and long dark hair that hung straight down the middle of her back. She could two-finger whistle a cab down from a block away. That night, she was wearing her favorite dress—a halter-top maxi, midnight blue swirled with purple clouds and moons—and platform sandals that made her taller than five-nine. At this point, my father still believed she was twenty-four years old and that her name was Alexis—both lies. She had heard hints of his past too. Only some of them turned out to be true. As they ate and talked, a cop in street clothes approached their table, with its bottle of wine and two glasses, flashed his badge, and asked to see her ID.

"I left my purse at home," she lied without hesitation.

The cop stared, unimpressed. Clearly, he suspected she was too young to be drinking on a date with this man who was old enough to be her parent. He must have noticed they weren't acting like father and daughter. Maybe he was part of the NYPD's recently formed Runaway Unit, tasked with keeping an eye out for minors who weren't supposed to be living on their own, grilling them for identification, and arresting them if their stories didn't line up. To a cop, she was a potential criminal. The graves of twenty-seven boys murdered by a serial killer in Houston, their disappearances initially written off as runaway cases, were still a year from being found. That discovery would lead to the Runaway Youth Act being passed in 1974, federal legislation designed to help, rather than criminalize, street kids. By then my mother had been married to Red for almost two years and my big brother was four months old. According to his birth certificate, she was nineteen when he was born. But that was a lie as well.

It all could have ended before any of that began. But my father was a practiced liar too.

"This is my wife," he said, a bold thing to say on a first date. The cop decided not to question it. A man in authority had been given a reason by another man not to care about a girl out of place. A reason was all he needed. He left them alone, and the story continued until it ended with my father's death, nine years and two children later.

Now, when I tell people the story of my family, their eyes round, they murmur "wow" with—what, exactly? Titillation? Maybe. Shock? Sometimes. They're naive, I used to tell myself. Conventional families are for other people, for those parents who met in college, at church, or at the office, who drove minivans to school pick-up, those people nobody could imagine ever being young.

The first time I questioned this understanding, I was sitting on a bed in a tiny hotel room in Manhattan in 2015, writing my reaction to new revelations from Mariel Hemingway about the making of *Manhattan*. My family's story, normal as it was to me, bore more than a passing resemblance to my erstwhile favorite movie, a once-celebrated auteur's romantic comedy classic now derided as the creepy wishcasting of a man who later pursued his own partner's college-aged daughter.

Have you ever held an obviously absurd belief for so long that once you see the truth clearly, you can only wish the ground would swallow you whole as punishment for being so pathetically oblivious?

Writing about it on the internet is the next best thing.

That morning, I was in New York on a three-day stay in a toile-decked theater district hotel close to my company's midtown office. Inside, it felt like I had stepped from the twenty-first century back into a film from the 1970s. The hotel lobby, shabby-elegant. The room, just shabby. No coffeemaker, which I took as an act of aggression. It was my first visit to the New York office since joining the staff of *Salon* six months earlier as a staff writer working remotely. Most of my coworkers lived in the city, and I wanted to meet them in person. After work the night before, I had gone out with a friend for wine and gossip and later had met my uncle for ramen. It had been a full day, and I was exhausted. As I let myself into my room, a breaking news alert popped up on my phone. Fox News had published an excerpt of Mariel Hemingway's new memoir that included an unflattering allegation about Allen's behavior after the filming of *Manhattan*: after she turned eighteen, he showed up at her home and tried to convince her to fly to Paris with him on what she finally understood was to be a lovers' getaway. Her parents encouraged her to go, and Hemingway was left to find her own strength to turn him down, which she did.

Hemingway's revelation came two and a half years before the Harvey Weinstein exposés blew #MeToo into prominence, but we were right in the thick of the multiple Bill Cosby sexual assault investigations as they were unfolding. I had written about my own experience interviewing Cosby—over the phone, thank god—and the misogyny I had encountered, and I had held myself accountable for not questioning him then about the allegations. I had also asked why the arts and entertainment press, myself included, had refused for so long to understand that they were also working a crime beat. The old media practices of treating misconduct allegations without formal charges, confessions, or convictions to substantiate them as gossip were starting to crumble, and the debate over the separation of (presumably valuable) art and the (allegedly reprehensible) artist was in full swing. Hemingway's account didn't allege any crimes, just unprofessional behavior that could be considered creepy. But it did make the "separate the art from the artist" argument that *Manhattan*'s admirers had leaned on for its cinematic respectability look awfully thin. There appeared to be precious little daylight between Allen and his protagonist. First, the artist hires a young girl, who has her first kiss with him on camera while she plays the role of the adoring and adorably eroticized, then exquisitely heartbroken, girlfriend. This is the art. And then, according to Hemingway, the artist waits the bare minimum of time for propriety's sake before trying to make his fantasy real.

I read the Hemingway excerpt in long gulps, knowing we would have to cover it. Half our readers would cheer their assumptions about Woody Allen being confirmed, and half would be incensed over the outrage being directed at one of their favorite geniuses and would defend him. As I opened my laptop to summarize the new revelations, I realized I couldn't write about the dismantling of Allen's gauzy fiction's plausible deniability—its lie—without also admitting that *Manhattan* had once been my favorite movie. This was almost a year after Dylan Farrow's open letter in the *New York Times* detailed her damning story of being sexually abused by Allen (allegations he denies), which I had originally—as a teenager in the 1990s reading the publicist-spun, incomplete narratives of the Farrow-Allen-Previn family rift in checkout-lane magazines hundreds of miles from New York City—misconstrued as an ambiguous claim in a bitter custody battle. After Dylan's letter, though, I could no longer see Allen's films as I once had. And yet I couldn't escape my own body of work, littered as it was with fond references to *Manhattan*, like one breezy story previewing an orchestra's Gershwin program with as many words devoted to Allen's use of *Rhapsody in Blue* in the film's opening monologue as to the composer himself. My brief commentary on Hemingway's shocking yet unsurprising story, and my own blind spots regarding the film, poured out of me in less than an hour. Writing it, I had to ask myself why I had loved this film and its objectionable pairing of Isaac with Tracy for so long. It was because I loved my mother and father and had believed for my whole life in the failed redemptive promise of their doomed romance.

"If I am confessing fully," I wrote that morning, fueled by a dusty can of lukewarm espresso, "I have to admit that on some level, I will always feel drawn to it, maybe in the way that disillusioned former churchgoers might feel a yearning from somewhere deep inside of them when they pass a door they know on so many levels they can never cross again. Knowing the truth about what you believe and longing for the time before you knew it are not mutually exclusive states of being."

In the years leading up to that day, I had watched and appreciated most of Allen's catalog through *Blue Jasmine*—even my maximalist tendencies couldn't convince me to sit through the entirety of *Anything Else,* and your guess is as good as mine as to the plot of *The Curse of the Jade Scorpion*—but usually, once was enough. Except *Manhattan.* I came back to it again and again, drawn to the guileless planes of Mariel Hemingway's voice, the ambivalent hunch of Diane Keaton's shoulders, Meryl Streep's exquisite thousand-yard stare, and Gordon Willis's immaculate camera work. Before I had many real-life models, I studied Keaton's character, Mary, for clues about how to be a writer in the world: how to be someone who called her editor, accepted book review assignments, attended museum galas, wielded her taste like a weapon, and had a complicated relationship with almost everyone—in other words, the person I thought I wanted to be. I didn't see that *Manhattan* was also a film that taught the winking away of "inappropriate" behavior under the umbrella of eccentricity, that laid the corroded framework for my own acceptance of things I otherwise might have questioned, like professors dating their eager students, or men with even a little bit of professional cachet pursuing women half their age because, as it was once explained to me, they lacked the emotional baggage age-appropriate women carried. My blasé acceptance of those power plays wasn't proof of my sophistication but rather my own naivete: *If it's consensual, who am I to judge?* My understanding of the dynamics and nuances of consent was shallow, uninformed.

I believed "no means no" but that anything less meant *sure*, that a girl was also a young woman, and that if she knew what she wanted, she should be allowed to pursue it. But *Manhattan* was also fiction, right? To make art that is true, we have to be willing to let characters do repugnant things, right? I told myself there was a bright line between art and reality and that everybody could see when that line was being crossed.

After that first date at the Captain's Table, things between Alexis and Red moved fast. She left the apartment she shared with her friend Judy on First Avenue and moved to Red's East Seventh Street apartment on the other side of Tompkins Square Park. It was crumbling and half-empty. Someone down the hall kept trying to kill himself with oven gas. Soon enough, Alexis realized she was pregnant with twins. Red needed a better job than driving a cab, something stable with regular hours. Michael lied to his boss and got Red in as a typesetter at the company where he worked. Four months into her pregnancy, my mother lost the babies. Maybe it was Red's Catholic guilt, or maybe it was his sense that life was short and he could see forty with a stable job and maybe—damn it—some kind of future that made sense and made his parents nod in approval, but he told Alexis that even though they didn't *have* to get married, he still thought they should. He had a way of saying things that made them sound true.

Her real age, though. That was a problem without parental consent, which she didn't have. She didn't have any identification proving she was old enough to get married. It could have all ended there. A girl who doesn't exist can't get married in the eyes of the church or state. But Alexis didn't like being at the mercy of the state's rules. There were all sorts of ways to get where you wanted to go if you couldn't get in through the front door. She knew a place, a storefront on Second Avenue, that sourced identification papers for underage kids. Nobody there would ask questions. The spirit of the Diggers' Free Store still lived in the Village at that time. There was a guy who gave her a blank baptismal certificate, proof the church would accept. She backdated her birth to say she was twenty-four, wrote down the name of the only priest she knew—her mother's old boss when she had worked as a secretary at a Benedictine monastery in Kansas—as the officiant. Michael from down the hall had a cousin who was a priest in Whitestone, Queens, who could perform a quick wedding service. And one day in November, they invited Red's close family—his parents; his younger sister, a nun; a cousin and his girlfriend—Alexis's old roommate Judy and Red's old roommate Kim, and their neighbor Michael. All the men wore ties except Red, who wore gray slacks and a black turtleneck that Alexis liked. She didn't want him in a suit.

My mother wore white, a body-skimming maxi dress with short sleeves and lace detail, dotted with delicate lilacs around the neckline and sleeves, and black heels. Her hair fell in loose chestnut waves around her shoulders. In the photos, she is surrounded by radiant, smiling friends, some of them maybe lightly buzzed. She looks like a girl being seen off by my excited family for a school dance. She is so clearly the youngest person in the room.

Maybe Red's parents had already guessed my mother was younger than twenty-four, that her backstory didn't quite line up with what they could see with their own eyes. But what good would it have done to ask questions at that point? A girl becomes permanent when a man appears next to her in the frame.

They drove back to Jersey City to Red's parents' apartment for a glass of wine and a piece of cake, and then the two of them borrowed his mother's car and drove to a little town in the Poconos where his parents had a modest vacation home. After a weekend honeymooning, they returned to the city and their newlywed lives.

In an essay for the *Paris Review*, "What Do We Do with the Art of Monstrous Men?," Claire Dederer excoriates *Manhattan*: "Woody Allen's usual genius is one of self-indictment, and here is his one film where that self-indictment falters, and also he fucks a teenager, and that's the film that gets called a masterpiece?" Writing about her anger at his horrifying pursuit of Soon-Yi Previn, his partner Mia Farrow's daughter whom he later married, Dederer explains that when she was young, she "felt like Woody Allen. I intuited or believed he represented me on-screen." I understand her feeling of betrayal, though I never thought of myself as Allen or any of his cinematic stand-ins. The female characters of *Manhattan* who so entranced me were still his creations, though, and I believed they were as complex as their male counterparts, a rare gift. But as Joanna E. Rapf notes her essay, "'It's Complicated, Really': Women in the Films of Woody Allen," while Allen "tries to give voice to female desire," his films ultimately serve a male perspective—namely, his own. "[H]is women are often extensions of himself and are seen through male eyes," she writes. Really, it wasn't any different from how I saw myself.

First, I gravitated toward Tracy, the prototypical Cool Girl, not realizing that what I saw as precocity was really a porousness, something malleable like the unfused plates in a baby's skull. As I got a little older, I identified with Mary, acolyte of genius male mentors, balancing paid commercial work with "little magazine" passion projects, independent of but still adjacent to men who are too in love with the vision they have of themselves and each other to have room for much of anyone else. Now, though I don't identify as queer,

I suppose I'm a Jill, the despised, vengeful she-writer who's penning a vulgar tell-all without using even fiction's flimsy robe for cover. But what took me so painfully long to understand is that *Manhattan* is not about these women, no matter how much conflict they present for Isaac to navigate.

After the film's iconic opening monologue and montage, the action opens inside Elaine's, underscored by jazz and background bustle, corduroy jackets and low light. How I fell for the aesthetics of it all, every trinket and accoutrement piled up to distract from a hollow center. This is what the life of a writer could be like, I felt—deep conversations with interesting people in vibrant cities where exciting things happen around every corner. Isaac and Tracy are there on a double date with Isaac's best friend Yale and Yale's wife, Emily. Isaac and Yale are having the same argument they've been having for years over the "essence of art." Yale maintains it serves "to provide a kind of working through situation for people so you can get in touch with feelings you didn't know you had." Isaac insists that talent is nothing but luck, that "the important thing in life is courage." Their conflict kicks off the film and, even when unspoken, animates it: Yale and Isaac's platonic romance—men revolving around each other—is the thing that really matters in *Manhattan*. Isaac first crushes on Mary when she's with Yale, an affair he helps Yale hide from Emily. And Mary doesn't break Isaac's heart by breaking up with him to go back to Yale. It's Yale who breaks Isaac's heart when he chooses Mary over their friendship. On the walk home from that opening date, Tracy and Emily—the ingenue and the wife, archetypes without much else to do—fade into the background when it's time for the men to open up to each other. When they get home and Emily tells Yale about Tracy—"I don't think seventeen is too young. Besides, she's a bright girl"—the audience is supposed to take the cue: find one woman to speak approvingly of a man's sexual transgression and he's pretty much in the clear.

Depicting mostly decent people who make bad choices and lie to themselves about it creates drama, and art can and should be about human flaws. Nonsupernatural humans, for those of us still interested in watching movies about them, rarely divide neatly along the lines of heroes and villains. But *Manhattan* frames Isaac as no more or less an unreliable narrator than anyone else; indeed, the culminating fight between him and Yale is over Isaac's sense of moral superiority. "You think you're god," Yale accuses, and Isaac fires back, "I have to model myself on someone." The scene following this argument, when Isaac realizes he wants Tracy back, is disingenuously positioned as a profound epiphany about what really matters in life.

Isaac's claim that Tracy is "God's answer to Job" imbues her with a divinity that is natural to aspire to possess. But it also, as Rapf notes, robs her of her humanity. "Tracy exists for Isaac on the surface," she writes. "He gestures towards her as he comments that in a world full of ugliness and pain, God 'can also make one of *these*,' a statement that denies Tracy's human complexity and turns her into an object."

In light of all that has been alleged to have unfolded in the fracturing of the Allen-Farrow-Previn family, *Manhattan*, once acclaimed as a classic and the director's best work, has now been recast as a piece of circumstantial evidence in the court of public opinion, part of Allen's long game of convincing his fans to see him as a truth-teller whose personal transgressions should be overlooked to preserve the value of his art. But in Allen's case, the claim about a separation between the art and artist has always been tenuous. As Caryn James wrote in a *New York Times* essay after the release of *Husbands and Wives*, the 1992 movie Allen and Farrow filmed as their romantic and professional relationship was crumbling, and which also features Allen in a romance with a much younger woman, Allen's blurring of the line between his characters and himself was "relentlessly" deliberate and appreciated by his fans: "Mr. Allen encouraged this confusion by using his own life as material, by displaying a modest public demeanor, by assuming the posture that we are all too sophisticated to confuse life and art."

And so there is also an argument to be made that *Manhattan* taught its audience to see men preying on teens as something that open-minded and sophisticated people—like movie stars, or their thinly spun fictional stand-ins, or the fans who identify with them— would accept or overlook, so long as the aesthetics of the relationship appealed to elite sensibilities. But that theory would give *Manhattan* too much credit. Isaac wasn't the first adult, fictional or real, famous or obscure, to sexually exploit his power over a girl. I gravitated toward *Manhattan* because my childish understanding of my parents' relationship groomed me to see this movie as a romance, not a shitshow. And I contributed to that normalization by glamorizing the story of my own mother's runaway past as a thrilling little adventure, by being unwilling to think deeply about how dangerous it must have been.

Was it Hollywood that taught me over and over again to hold limitless sympathy for flawed men and their conflicted desires while also maintaining strict rules about "likability" for girls and women? Or was it real life that hammered that lesson home? I think of the eager White House intern and the brilliant president, how the cultural narratives at the time juxtaposed a great man's moment of weakness against a young girl's scheming grab for attention. I think of the writer who auctioned off the seduction letters written to her when she was barely out of high school by the reclusive genius novelist twice her age, how her peers demanded she protect his privacy so that their innocence regarding him could be preserved. How recent and tenuous a narrative victory it is that a woman could be as real, as deserving of her own version of the story, as a beloved and flawed man. In fact, it is Woody Allen's "personal imperfection" that "makes him more human and real," scholar Sam Girgus posits. I'm going to be a little unfair here to Girgus, an astute critic and scholar, by cherry-picking a quote of his about Tracy for comparison: "a truly original character" who nevertheless sounds like nothing more than any average middle-aged man's flat fantasy, "a young woman who becomes a blending of romanticized feminine adoration, vulnerable innocence, and unselfish sophistication." To my eye, though, this accurately reflects how her character is written. Tracy's worth is not found in her agency and interiority. She is reduced to her beauty and willingness to bend.

But Allen's celebrated aesthetics—white, affluent, erudite, impeccably lit and scored—soothed his fans into letting Isaac get away with it. With Isaac's epiphany at the end, in which he places the human girl Tracy in the same list of stuff that make life worth living—such as Cézanne's pears, the comedy of Groucho Marx, or Flaubert's *Sentimental Education* (we see what you did there, Woody!)—*Manhattan* seals its approval of the Isaac-Tracy affair as, above all, a matter of taste. Those of us seduced by that aesthetic should thank Joan Didion for devastatingly roasting us for falling for a high-school-level caricature of adult sophistication. As she puts it, Allen's praised wit is actually "meaningless, and not funny . . . smart talk meant to convey the message that the speaker knows his way around Lit and History," culminating in a list she dismisses as "the ultimate consumer report." In other words, liking the crabs at Sam Wo's is not a personality. The film's characters, Didion writes in her scathing 1979 essay, "Letter from *Manhattan*," are "sentient men and women in the most productive years of their lives, but their concerns and conversations are those of clever children, 'class brains,' acting out a yearbook fantasy of adult life." The exception, she points out, is the only actual child of the bunch, Tracy, herself a fantasy kid with an adult life and no visible parents. Rapf highlights Tracy as the character in *Manhattan* who changes the most. The more I think about it, that might be the most honest thing in Allen's film. She's only seventeen, for Christ's sake. She's supposed to be changing as fast as she can grow.

———————————

After writing about the Mariel Hemingway revelation, I found myself taking on more stories like it as a writer and an editor, drawing on my own history of indulging the beloved flawed-man narrative. Every time I turned around, another story about a powerful man and an underage girl or otherwise vulnerable young woman appeared— from the creepy to the complex to the outright criminal—layered in alongside the explosive #MeToo trials of Harvey Weinstein, Bill Cosby, and R. Kelly, all of which demanded coverage. After David Bowie's death, even—an incomparable genius, mine and seemingly everyone's idol—his reported early-career sex with teen groupies was a live wire few wanted to touch. I wrote about the complexities of acknowledging it as part of his story, hiding from the internet's reactionary wrath for a full two weeks after filing. Stories about older men pursuing or dating teenage girls emerged from every corner of the entertainment industry. How many people had to look the other way when girls crossed paths with men who believed they were entitled to pursue them? Didn't those girls deserve the safety of their own soft, frustrated dreams instead?

I wrote about goddamn Woody Allen again, coming back for rounds two and three, first when a former model alleged that she had been the real-life Tracy to his Isaac, and again when he and Soon-Yi agreed to a rare and bizarre magazine profile, a story choice my boss puzzled over in a meeting of mostly men after my commentary on the profile didn't get enough clicks. ("Nobody was really talking about that story," he explained. But who was "nobody"? Every woman I followed online, it seemed, had thoughts about the profile.) The exploitation and degradation of women and girls is at once an urgently necessary and a demoralizing and unrelenting beat, made all the more frustrating when the gauge of how much the world should care about each individual story is measured in page views.

After every damning allegation comes the question of those beloved albums, those influential movies, those stand-up specials, those groundbreaking television shows—all the artifacts fans reexamine in a new light. It all boils down to the question we're all sick of but can't escape: Can you separate the art you loved from what you now think about the artist, even if the artist spent his entire career flirting with that line's erasure? That question is not about reading autobiography into novels or films or lyrics but rather one of guilt-free consumption: Can any piece of art be good, or at least morally neutral, if it was made by a bad person for questionable reasons? Can't we just continue to enjoy things we no longer approve of for old time's sake? Especially when the art in question is designed to appeal to those who think of themselves as people who aren't drawn to shallow celebrities but to true artists? James's observation that *Husbands and Wives* resembled the real-life Allen/Farrow celebrity scandal could, and should, be made about *Manhattan*, too: "Most chilling of all, people who saw themselves in the good old Woody can't shake off the identification just because it turned unpleasant."

It is embarrassing to see the things and people you once idolized now widely regarded as tragic or grotesque, especially when you finally see it that way for yourself. There is a loneliness to it, realizing the joke's been on you the whole time. In the case of *Manhattan*, though, it's not only the metanarrative around the film and the way Allen so lightly treats Isaac and Tracy's age disparity that are troubling in hindsight. There's also a sleight of hand at work on the female characters in Isaac's life. Allen creates these richly drawn, intriguing, intense, infuriating women and then spends much of the movie humiliating them. And what are we to make of that?

First, Yale passes Mary to Isaac like a worn-out toy, then he shamelessly parades Emily in front of her on their double dates. That Emily still doesn't know by the end of the film that Yale's affair with Mary predated her relationship with Isaac is humiliating for her. The audience can see that she still believes his lies, and the movie doesn't seem to care if Isaac's silence is supposed to be restraint or cowardice. And Jill, supposedly taking Isaac down a peg or two with her emasculating tell-all, is reduced, even in her memoir's title— *Marriage, Divorce, and Selfhood*—to a woman who can't move on from him, artistically at least. The repeated anecdote about Isaac's attempt to run over Jill's lover with his car is played as a gag—we're meant to roll our eyes at the couple's overreaction to it—not an indictment of Isaac's capacity for violence against women, which they relive every time he picks up their son for a visit. And then there's Tracy, dumped at a soda fountain, the camera close on her face with Isaac's hand still in the shot, caressing her cheek, her neck. That disconnected hand, her weeping face. "Leave me alone," she pleads as he murmurs off-screen, "Hey, come on, don't cry, Tracy, come on Tracy, Tracy, don't cry." And then at the end, she's punished for wanting to move on after he has told her to do so. Isaac's long run to Tracy's apartment to catch her before she leaves for London is shown as heroic not pathetic, a return to "the little girl," as Mary called her, after having his heart broken by Yale. "I would prefer it if you didn't go," he tells her as the doorman loads her bags in the car. (Everyone wants a free girl until they don't want her to be free anymore.) The film feints like it's giving Tracy the last word—"You have to have a little faith in people"—but doesn't that just put a promise in her mouth that she will return from London as the same person, to Isaac presumably, instead of shedding him like a strange episode she should by rights have the opportunity to grow beyond? Because the script has positioned her as one of the few uncompromised things on Earth that make life worth living, this promise only confirms her goodness, and therefore the goodness of such a pledge.

What can I say about knowing every inch of this movie and loving it anyway for as long as I did? That I craved those vicarious humiliations? That I needed to be reminded, in such gorgeous shots, that I can't trust what I'm seeing? That it could be comforting to be told that I would be misinterpreting Allen's intent to see it that way, that I'd be unfairly accusing him, that women and girls can't and shouldn't be trusted to be the center of such stories?

On the day I finally saw *Manhattan* as a corrosive fantasy, I began to see my parents' marriage in a different light. I saw my father as the adult, the one who should have made wiser choices, just as Isaac should never have dated Tracy in the first place (a proposition *Manhattan* never seriously entertains). Remember Yale's wife, Emily, the feminine nurturer, declaring breezily, "She's a bright girl"? That line doesn't just serve to normalize the terms of the relationship for the audience. It's not even delivered with that much power, relative to the philosophical arguments that preoccupy *Manhattan*'s characters. The line's casualness signals a troubling truth: Emily, the least transgressive of the main characters, is just echoing a norm she's absorbed. In the real world, Isaac and Tracy together would be a minor scandal, but only if Tracy made it one. She's a bright girl, after all. She understands how the world works.

Can I wish my mother had been rerouted somehow to a safe and whole adolescence, to college, to medical school, and to whatever might have come after that instead of to that church in Queens? Can I do that without regretting my own existence? I'll admit this is approaching Woody Allen-levels of narcissism, but as a thought exercise, this question troubles me precisely because I spent so long never even thinking to ask it. "Your father, oh, he loved you more than anything," my mother always told me. That seemed like just enough to excuse what led to that love I craved so acutely for its absence.

On social media today, my father would be labeled a sex offender, a predator, or worse. That is not the precise truth of my parents' relationship as either of them understood it. Terms like that can be useful and convenient. They flatten our understanding of a man "dating" a teenage girl into a simple act of individual criminal pathology while dismissing the culpability of an entire culture that has enabled and even encouraged it. And yet there is a need to name it as wrong, to keep seeking deeper understandings and precise terms about power and vulnerability that we currently lack.

My mother does not consider herself a victim—not of my father; not of the other men who exploited her vulnerability during those years; and not of her parents who, in my opinion, didn't fight hard enough to keep her safe. And yet the world has now decided that she must have been one. I can't label her as such. What I can say is every girl deserves to live as a girl, not as an adult before she is one, for no other reason than the fact of her humanity, which as a culture we are still quick to find reasons to discard: she looked older, she wanted it, she shouldn't have been talking to grown men in the first place, she knew what she was getting into. A bright girl learns early there are three ways to hear those words: first as praise, then as a threat, and finally as a taunt.

In a 2018 profile in the *Hollywood Reporter*, Babi Christina Engelhardt, a former teen model, claimed to have been a real-life Tracy to Allen in the 1970s, a *Manhattan* muse. They kept their affair a secret, she said, because Allen, who did not comment for the article, was worried about her age and his reputation. A subway ride away at the time, my parents lived openly in the ramshackle apartment my mother was too ashamed to invite her parents to visit, and nobody around them said a word. Like my mother, Engelhardt is resistant to having her younger self be judged in hindsight. But as Engelhardt rewatched *Manhattan*, she asked what kind of a movie it would have been if Tracy's story had been foregrounded instead. "It's a remake I'd like to see," she told the reporter.

What genre would Tracy's movie be if a woman wrote the ending? A tragicomedy? True crime? *Manhattan* is Isaac's story, and it always will be. But even if I could wipe away my history with Allen's film, revise my relationship to it with a gender-flipped perspective, I'm not sure I would want to. I'm afraid I'd forget what I once thought I knew about Tracy's face and how he saw it.

In the faded Kodachrome prints of my parents' wedding, I see what the photographers saw and wanted the world to see: a bride, a husband, a small family, and a clutch of close friends there to lend their approval and support. In those photographs, I see their answer to my father's history with addiction, his arrest record, his inability to thrive in the straight life and continue an upwardly mobile path that he had, before that moment, resisted at every turn. In the same way that Tracy functions as Isaac's existential redemption prize, my grandparents thought getting married would settle him, give him something to better himself for. At the same time, I see the twisted wishful thinking and relief when an unruly girl gets domesticated. I hear her father in the background of the phone call she finally made, three months after the photos were taken, to tell her mother she wasn't coming home ever again because she was married. "Thank God," her father roared, "we don't have to worry about her anymore."

Watching *Manhattan* all those years, I knew in my heart why Isaac lists Tracy's face as one of the few things that make life worth living. He believes she had been created to redeem the pain of existence for him. One of the lies I had told myself about my father, and one I had believed for so long, was that that had been our job too. Our existence—my mother and the family and home she made for him—was supposed to save him. So it must have been our fault when it didn't. When I could finally see my parents' marriage from the outside, in the same light I saw Tracy and Isaac's relationship, I began to see not only how much of my identity had been built on that lie but also how much ambient reinforcement that lie had been given from the culture around me. And now I had questions my father wasn't alive to answer and maybe never would have asked himself.

2
Earl-Aye in the Morning

The first time I interviewed my mother, I was writing an essay for Father's Day about my attempts to understand how a man decides to marry a girl young enough to be his daughter, a person not even old enough to legally drive, and how the world around him allows it. He was already dead, so she was my primary source for reconstructing the night they met, their first date, and how they fell in love. I felt vaguely uneasy writing so nakedly about him in the first place. The "daddy issues" label hovered menacingly off-page. I thought I could approach it like a reporter, but I knew I had no objectivity on the story. I did have an agenda, though: to understand exactly what I could hold him accountable for so I could put my survivor's guilt to rest. But by the time I finished writing that essay, what was left was a deep curiosity about *her* story, everything I realized I didn't know that led up to her meeting him in that bar and going with him to that restaurant and all that came after.

And yet the mystery of my father's life nagged at me. I didn't like that I had more questions than answers. I still needed to understand how he ended up on that date with a girl who was clearly so young so I could understand exactly who she fell in love with. It's an old habit I fell back into—the desire to explain him, to craft a narrative for him that we could fit into. The belief that past must be prequel was a hard one to shake.

The truth is, I had holes in my memory where he should have been, and I had filled in those gaps with my own imagined flourishes for so long I didn't know what was true and what was make-believe. I can't recall the sound of his voice and can only barely form the impressions of still images where he is the focus, rather than my mother, brother, grandparents, friends, or neighbors. It's like a digital file that got corrupted; only chance pixels remain. Overall, my memory didn't become reliable until right after his death, as if a switch flipped. There are no home movies, no recordings of his voice. Only albums upon albums of photographs, a handful of letters, and a few artifacts my mother rescued from his meager possessions at the time of his death.

Here is what little I knew about my father, other than the facts of his birth, death, and family. He had strong opinions about movies and books—*The Lord of the Rings, Young Frankenstein,* both recommended texts—that he wasn't shy about sharing. A critic's impulses run in my blood. He loved his album of sea shanties, singing, "What will we do with a drunken sailor, earl-aye in the morning?" Perhaps this was an act of self-interrogation; his methadone-managed abstention from heroin did not extend to full sobriety, and he drank Budweiser by the case. ("Put him in the bed with the captain's daughter" is one suggested solution, yo ho ho.) I inherited his love of reading and Irish music, along with his green tweed flat cap with a busted bill that I can't bear to let out of my sight long enough to be repaired; *The Collected Works of William Shakespeare,* with his and my mother's names inscribed, my closest analog to a family Bible; a red bandanna worn thin with age; and a yellow- and orange-embroidered camera strap I now use to carry a purse. He also gave me the same set of bruise-dark under-eye circles I see staring back at me from every photo he's in, including the one of us together when I was maybe seven or eight months old.

He grew up not working too hard in school despite the value his parents put on education. He assumed he'd one day own the family filling station his father ran near what's now Liberty State Park in Jersey City, but it didn't play out like that, and the family business had to be sold. Maybe my father never got over a case of thwarted entitlement, the nagging feeling that life had promised him something it did not deliver. Maybe he didn't know who he wanted to be once he had to build a life himself.

I knew he had spent time in jail, though exactly for what was bit of a mystery. Maybe drugs or stealing. He called it "boosting," my mother told us—packing fur coats from department stores in the false bottoms of suitcases in the days before sophisticated theft-prevention technology. He was an excellent shot, trained in the Marines as a marksman, but he mostly just hit empty cans for target practice. What always got waved away as unknown was what he was doing in the decade between leaving the Marines and hearing the woman he was in love with confess to him that she was actually ten years younger than she had told him she was. "Well, shit," my mother remembers him saying, "that sucks." But he didn't break up with her. He married her anyway.

My mother told me the story of that moment during our first interview. There's a time in every story when a choice changes everything, a moment that in hindsight becomes a beginning. The choice you focus on determines whose story you're going to tell.

I am alive because my father met a girl in a bar and sang her songs, recited her poems, talked about books he had read and places he'd been, and was admired for it. My mother met a man in a bar and drew herself up to her full height. She told the world a story about herself too. Nobody knew the whole truth of that moment, or at least nobody cared. "It was a different time," we say now about men and girls and then and now, and the choices we linger on and those we forget or forgive. But we are still finding ways to tell women their stories matter less than those of the men they affect.

Before our interview, I had never asked my mother about anything that had come before or after that moment the two of them met in the bar-light glow, a still from a film I had never seen. "Your father, he loved you kids," she would skip ahead in the story, because she knew I was really asking about him, because he's all I've ever wanted to know about. "I've never seen anyone as in love with anyone as he was with you and your brother." She had crafted the myth of my father and passed it down to us, a legacy of romantic ruin, a fairy tale I wanted to believe in because it was echoed in beloved stories all around me: a man of large appetites that eventually destroyed him after he thought he had survived the calamities that had driven him to excess. The father I lost had a pirate's heart, a poet's soul. She was reluctant to disturb my restless dream.

How could I hold him accountable when I didn't even know the basics of who he was? The concrete details my reporter's brain craved— dates, locations, convictions, circumstances, documentation—to counteract my worst poetic impulses, he took to the grave. I didn't know how to let him go, but I did know how to look for information. I started with a handful of records requests, standard practices. And one day, answers arrived.

New York can be glorious in early October, especially on warm days when the temperature breaks seventy degrees, the sky a clear and piercing blue, the trees just hinting at their impending transformation to golden fire. On such a day in 1962, a twenty-six-year-old Red, with a round face and twinkling blue eyes, may have seen such a clear sky as a US Marshal transported him from the federal detention center on West Street downtown to the Foley Street federal courthouse to appear for his sentencing before the Honorable David N. Edelstein in the Southern District Court of New York.

This was my father's first time in front of Judge Edelstein since his arrest on August 30; after a grand jury indictment, he had pleaded guilty to four counterfeiting charges to a different judge, the Honorable Archie O. Dawson. It appears to be Red's first felony arrest and first federal case after a handful of small busts, the exact number and nature of which are hard to determine.

"He is a fine-looking young man," his Legal Aid lawyer, Bernard Moldow, told the judge. "He has several convictions in connection with narcotics. I think the most time he ever served was ninety days. And in July of this year, recognizing his problem and having some insight, he voluntarily committed himself to the hospital at Lexington. And that was about where his good judgment ended, because six days later he signed himself out."

I looked at a printout of my father's case file and transcripts from federal court, retrieved and scanned and emailed to me by the angels who work in the National Archives. I had submitted a request for any records that included his name and birthdate, dated anytime in the 1960s. This inquiry was based on pure speculation. I didn't know what, if anything, would turn up.

I knew what he had told my mother, who passed the stories down to my brother and me after he died. These made up our apocrypha, the *Book of Red*. As a small child, the story went, he was one of the last remaining smallpox cases on the Eastern seaboard, and he spent months in quarantine recovering, where nobody from his family, including his parents, was allowed to visit. After high school, he joined the Marines and saw overseas action in Operation Blue Bat during the 1958 Lebanon crisis. At some point after that, he found himself marooned on the Canary Islands for six months—how or why was never explained, but the implication was always criminal—where he learned to speak fluent Spanish with "a beautiful Castilian accent" before eventually making his way back stateside. In the 1960s, he became addicted to heroin. He joined New York City's methadone program in the early 1970s and had been clean for about a year when he met my mother.

These scant details I had of my father's life metastasized into a myth for me as a child. I came to believe quarantine isolation traumatized him at an early age, making him more susceptible as an adult to seek out drugs and alcohol, as did his military service in a foreign intervention few remembered. His drug abuse led him into the underworld, where he put his military training to work on illegal operations that got him to the Canary Islands and then stranded him there. A little boy locked away in a room who became a tortured combat veteran and then a brash smuggler—a dark fairy tale from start to finish. I filled in the blank spots with my own embellishments, my father's most loyal collaborator in spinning his bullshit tales from beyond the grave.

But he wasn't a fairy-tale hero or villain. I realized, when faced with the gaps in the record, I could treat him like the subject of any story I needed background on. He was a man with a birthdate, a social security number, and even, in a Long Island military cemetery I've never visited, a grave. It was somewhere to start.

I tackled the smallpox story first, and it turned out to be the easiest one to strike. A simple internet search and one phone call was all it took. The last smallpox outbreak in the US happened in New York City in 1947, according to *New York Times* coverage concerning how the city mobilized a mass vaccination effort—five million people inoculated in two weeks—with a robust publicity campaign and thousands of civilian volunteers administering shots. My father was born in 1936, which would have made him eleven years old at that point if his case *had* coincided with this notorious outbreak. He would have been nowhere near "the final patient." And even if he had been an outlier case several years earlier, in Jersey City where his family lived, it is doubtful that a boy who spent most of his time within a mile radius of his home on Bayside Avenue would have been the sole member of the family, or their close-knit Irish Catholic community, to contract such a contagious disease. It was simply a lie. What he had was chicken pox. A particularly severe case, according to my aunt, for which he was briefly hospitalized, for a week or so, in what we estimated would have been 1944, when he was seven or eight.

"Of course he had visitors. Our parents were allowed in," she told me. "I remember getting ice cream after, for being good while I waited in the car, because they didn't want me to get it yet. I was too young."

His Marine service records confirmed the provenance of the scars he had brought with him into the military. I had sent off for those details, botching the job at first by accidentally requesting the wrong files, the ones that only gave the type of outline information sought by amateur genealogists. The second request netted me a fat envelope for the next of kin, though, and in those records, another lie surfaced. The furthest from home my father ever got during his nearly three years of active duty was basic training in Parris Island, followed by a post at Camp Lejeune in North Carolina. The page in his service record labeled "Expeditions—Engagement—Combat Record" was blank save his name and serial number. "Sea and Air Travel Embarkation Slips," same. The Beirut story? Invented, it seems, out of thin air: He had been released from active duty three months before President Eisenhower authorized the 1958 military intervention.

I had been so desperate for the sympathetic narrative I had created to explain my father's life, the conditions that would have affected his emotional stability to a point that he would later make the decision to marry my mother even after learning how young she was, that I had waited decades to seek out basic information on what he might have actually experienced.

The most telling information my father's service records offered was something I already knew: his diagnosis of acute gastritis, which persisted into his postmilitary life and eventually, exacerbated by alcohol abuse, turned into internal bleeding and killed him. My aunt now believes he was prescribed pain medication for his condition after he was discharged, and as it did for millions of Americans, pain management started him on the road to dependency, which led him to illegal narcotic use and addiction. That's plausible. And indirectly, heroin was how he came to be standing in a Southern District courtroom in 1962.

When I got to the part in the court transcript where his lawyer mentioned the hospital in Lexington, I sucked in my breath. That was just seventy miles from where I live now, and I never knew my father had even been to Kentucky.

A month after the first time Red signed himself out of the United States Public Health Service Center in Lexington, Kentucky—colloquially known as the Narco Farm—he met with his codefendant, a man no one in our family had ever heard of, to start the scheme that landed them in the custody of Special Agent Charles L. Gittings of the US Treasury Department on August 30, 1962, charged with four counts involving the possession of and attempt to pass counterfeit twenty-dollar bills, a quick gamble to fund his heroin habit, which he had quickly returned to after leaving the Farm.

"This is a common error; many addicts do this," his lawyer continued. "As soon as they have gone through withdrawal and they have had a little help from the medical people through that very difficult stage, they think they have the problem in hand and they can solve their future. And experience tells us that isn't enough."

Moldow asked Judge Edelstein to give Red a second chance at rehab with a mandatory stint at the Narco Farm, which the US Department of Public Health ran as both a prison and a voluntary addiction treatment facility. Founded as a working farm in 1935 on 1,050 acres outside Lexington, it was the first center of its kind for drug addicts, who prison wardens wanted very much to keep out of their own facilities. Famous alumni who took "the Lexington Cure" included William S. Burroughs, who wrote about it in his 1953 semi-autobiographical novel *Junky*, and Rat Packer Sammy Davis Jr. So many accomplished musicians, including Sonny Rollins, Ray Charles, and Chet Baker, had been there that the facility even had its own band. Jazz musicians learned from each other at Lexington; they checked in and enjoyed the free time and the suspension of the outside world's duties and pressures, which allowed them to focus on making music together. It was a means of therapy that crossed both work and play, two areas the Lexington staff believed helped with rehabilitation.

The Narco Farm also housed the Addiction Research Center, where doctors studied the physical and psychological effects different drugs had on volunteer inmate addicts who signed up to be given narcotics and have their reactions—and their withdrawal symptoms—monitored. New pharmaceuticals were also tested on inmates to determine their side effects, addictive properties, and dangers. Between 1953 and 1962, the year Red was first admitted, the Narco Farm also provided the CIA with a captive population for its secret MK-ULTRA mind-control experiments using LSD and other drugs. Patients were even given drugs as payment for participating in the experiments. In 1975, after coming under scrutiny for its history of experimenting on prisoners, the Narco Farm closed; the facility is now a federal prison for inmates who need medical or psychiatric care. But in the early 1960s, it was simultaneously Red's best chance to get clean, given the resources that were available, and an incredibly challenging environment for him to actually do so, with most former patients relapsing "almost immediately" upon leaving, according to a 1962 study.

"The atmosphere at Lexington, from what I saw in the place in the brief time I was there, it is not conducive to breaking the drug habit," Red told Judge Edelstein during his October 1962 sentencing hearing. "It's just an arresting phase or something. Of course, I haven't gone through any psychotherapy or anything like that, so I don't really know."

I studied the court transcript of my father's address to the court like a monk with an illuminated scroll. I had his voice captured in letters, where he could toil over every word, choosing his phrasing carefully. We're a family of obsessive photographers, so I also have plenty of snapshots of my father through the ages: a baby-faced, snazzy young man in skinny tie and suit with my aunt in full habit after she took her vows in the order of the Sisters of Charity; a barrel-chested and bearded dad in a Fair Isle knit and a green tweed cap. I had no extemporaneous record of his spoken voice, though. And now I could finally hear him, in a way, in court, vulnerable and humbled, likely physically and emotionally drained from detoxing in the West Street jail, putting himself at the mercy of a federal judge, having to explain why rehab had not helped him kick the addiction that had led to him passing counterfeit bills. Even in a weakened state, he was confident enough to issue sweeping statements on the efficacy of a federal institution, savvy enough to signal his willingness to engage with another kind of court-mandated therapy as an alternative to incarceration. A daughter is not supposed to hear her father like this, trying to convince a judge to give him a way out. But as a journalist, I'd heard worse. Red's voice in the court transcript, seeking both sympathy and absolution, had much in common with so many men's carefully wrought statements I've read and written about. I knew how this story went. He was a fine-looking young white man with a good vocabulary who recognized his problems. The court would, of course, give him another chance.

While Judge Edelstein understood that no one treatment could promise 100 percent efficacy, he appears to have believed in a kind of face-your-demons approach, that it was better for an addict to have to work to prevail. Red's sentence included a return to Lexington for a court-ordered stay—six to nine months, or however long it took for doctors to deem him cured—followed by two years of probation.

"If you are concerned about association with others at Lexington that you may know, and you are concerned about the influence they are going to have upon you, let me tell you, you might just as well come to grips with it now," Edelstein said. "Because all your life, regardless of what level of society you occupy, whether it is you or Mr. Moldow or anybody in this court, you can be sure that temptations beset us at every turn in the road. If you are going to lick this and make something of your life, you have got to lick it in spite of all the temptations that come your way."

"Yes, sir," Red said.

"I suppose the most certain way of keeping a man pure, clean and honest is to isolate him, put him in solitary confinement, and bar him in, and then there is a fair and reasonable chance that he can avoid indiscretions. But you have exercise of free will. I know that sounds simple, but it isn't. You have to learn to use that free will. And I think, after a fashion, it is a little bit like anything else: it has to be used to become strong, and it has to be used against opposing forces to become firm."

If Edelstein had talked to more of the 96 percent of patients who reportedly relapsed after leaving Lexington, he might have made a different decision. But like the doctors at the Narco Farm and the US

Public Health Department itself, he likely didn't know any better at the time. And he was, at least by my reading of his remarks in court, a generous man who by his own admission believed in miracles.

Red was delivered to the Narco Farm on October 31, 1962. By August 2 the following year, a new warrant had been issued for his arrest for absconding and failing to check in with his probation officer. He was taken into custody in Chelsea at West Nineteenth Street and Eighth Avenue, near the sleek, Art Moderne-designed Elgin Theater that, at that point, still played Spanish-language films. This time in court, Red pulled the Honorable Irving Ben Cooper, whom he asked to remand him once again to the Narco Farm.

"When I came out of Lexington this time I had a lot of self-confidence, and a few things went wrong for me and I lost sight of the type of patient I was and I reverted to the use of drugs. I think if I can get back and get myself in that frame of mind again and try again, maybe not in New York or near New York for a while, I think I can make it."

The judge pressed him on his conviction for recovery, threatening him with the full weight of a twenty-year federal sentence.

"Don't think we are soft little boys, because we are not," Judge Cooper chided. "We see cases by the thousands. We see people in the raw. We look at them as though they are naked. We are not hardened creatures. I will give you a chance, and this is the last chance."

He issued one final warning: "No judge is going to touch you with a ten-foot pole if you two-time us again."

And yet on April 14, 1964, it was discovered that Red had gone missing again. A new warrant was issued, but this time he was harder to find. He was eventually discovered at Lyons Hospital, a VA medical facility in New Jersey, checked in as a patient. Then, sometime after June 16, he absconded from the hospital and was arrested on September 25, just a few blocks up Eighth Avenue from his last bust.

In October, he attempted to explain his decisions to a final judge, the Honorable Edward Weinfeld:

> I feel that if I had at this time close supervision—what I meant by that was, I have a close contact with my probation officer now. I am out of contact with my family, and I feel this is beneficial to me, because there is a pull between myself and my family. When I am away from them, I can make decisions myself, and I can more or less guide myself to do what I want to do. While I am with them, it turns out that I do just what they don't want me to do, whether I want to do it myself or not. But I thought if I could have close supervision by the Probation Department, and I have enrolled in an after-care plan at Greenwich House for out-patient therapy—I did that myself—I thought there might be a chance for me to lick my narcotics addiction.

A theme recurs in all Red's addresses to the court. In these transcripts, he is articulate and reflective to a point but not especially accountable. He says he wants to be away from the New York area, away from his parents whose expectations and disappointment he rebelled against like a child. He believes that will transform him into a person who can finally conquer his addiction. But then he gravitates back to the same spots, where his old life is always waiting for him. He's not denying his illness nor what he's done because of it, but these are also the words of a man who has told himself that his problems always start with someone or something else.

"The judgment I am going to impose upon you is one where I view you as a sick person and not a criminal, even though you have committed a crime, in the hope that you will get some help," Judge Weinfeld told Red before denying his request to return to Lexington and resume his probation. He instead reinstated Red's original two-year prison sentence. "I am not going to recommend that you go to Lexington. That has not helped you as much as it has been hoped it would help."

Something must have changed between the judge's remarks in court and Red's transfer to prison, though, because the court documents end with a form directing a US marshal to deliver him to the Narco Farm after all. The next record I found was a letter he wrote to his sister dated September 1967, three years after that final court date, from the federal prison in Danbury, Connecticut, where he had one month left to serve in his two-year sentence. Perhaps somewhere in that lost year, between the Narco Farm and Danbury, lies the answer to the Canary Islands.

The story my aunt told me is that he ran off, but to where she didn't really know. She had taken her vows in the Sisters of Charity of Elizabeth order, and she'd been living at the Catholic orphanage where she taught. She was a bit disconnected from family drama. And when Red's mother went to pick him up at the airport, law enforcement was also there, and he was taken away in handcuffs. Was he being transported by plane back to New York from Lexington, after detoxing and getting clean, so he wouldn't abscond on the way to serving out his prison sentence? Or had he been intercepted upon his return from an overseas scheme that had left him marooned off the coast of Morocco until he could finagle a flight home? *Put him in a long boat til he's sober*, as the sea shanty goes. I can collect any number of stories to fill in that time, but without documentation, they all trace back to one unreliable narrator.

———————————

There are facts about my father I can prove now that help separate myth from reality. But nestled inside the documents that fill in those facts are also truths about him I didn't know. From his letter from prison, I learned what kinds of straight work might have appealed to him once he was released: He didn't want to be a cog in the system. Maybe social work, so he could help others. He never did this. He was also full of confident recommendations—proud of the books he'd read, of learning to paint. He was especially proud of his painted copy of a *Time* magazine cover portrait of Irish playwright Brendan Behan. That painting is lost, but another he made while in prison, a Swedish Falu red farmhouse—his grandmother's home back in the Åland Islands, which he had never seen himself—hangs above my desk in my home office, a reminder of his attempts and mine to make something meaningful, something that can last, even if it is only an interpretation of someone else's memory.

Now, when the state lottery jackpot swells to the hundreds of millions, I play a serial number from one of my father's counterfeit bills, mostly for the chance to tell a good story if it wins. I am still his daughter. Of course, the number never hits.

A few months after I received the court transcripts, I took a long lunch on a work trip and visited New York City's criminal courts archives, searching for his name in the microfiche records between October 1967, when he was released from Danbury, and May 1972, when he met my mother and their story began. Nothing turned up. There are still plenty of empty spaces, but seeing the pattern repeat itself through five years of revolving-door treatment and incarceration, I am disinclined to create interesting possibilities to fill in those blanks. Most likely it was more of the same cycle of actively using and being in treatment until he wound up in methadone maintenance and finally broke free of heroin in 1971.

A month after I went to the archives, my mother visited for Christmas. I laid out the documents I had gathered, passed her folders of papers to thumb through, and went down the list of proof: chicken pox, no Beirut, the Narco Farm, the federal case, the final bid in Danbury. The paperwork revealed small details, like the fact that he had gone to college after all—one semester at Saint Peter's, the Jesuit university near his house in Jersey City, which my aunt confirmed after I noticed it on his Marine personnel form—though the family joke had always been that he was an alum of Rikers Island. In that detail, I saw a different future for him, one that didn't end up on an endless loop on the same block of Eighth Avenue.

My mother shook her head.

"I can't believe he just lied about it all," she said, even though "Your father, he lied a lot" was a worn mantra in our family, just as familiar as "Your father, he loved you."

"Wow," she kept saying to me. "There was a lot I didn't know."

I considered the fact that she didn't tell him she had lied about her age until after they had fallen in love. I considered the truth that a fifteen-year-old girl will believe most things a man she loves tells her. Two people met and fell in love with each other's fabricated identities. After years of scrutiny by his family and the courts, maybe Red welcomed the space to construct a different version of himself for someone who might believe it. Leave some blanks. Let her fill them in with a man she could believe in. In return, she extended him the same grace she sought for herself: the gift of not looking too closely, of not asking any pointed questions, of letting him be who he said he was and nobody else.

She did eventually come clean with him. His confessions never came, though. I had to get them from the authorities. I had to lay out the reports in the glow of the Christmas tree lights, put his own words back in his mouth, trace every fact documented in each record while telling her, and myself: *Look, here, finally, facts and proof. His pain was real, and it was common. His scars were not special after all.*

What should we do with a drunken sailor? The number of verses sung with gusto in the traditional shanty suggests a bottomless

stamina for centering the problems of the problem man. I laughed
the day it hit me, listening to the song on repeat. My mother was the
runaway in the family; that was her role. So what did this record I
had of Red's run-ins with the authorities, of breaking probation by
disappearing into the underworld, not to mention his wild tale of lost
months in the Canary Islands, make him?

3
Jersey Girls

Once I got it in my head to go visit the girl skeleton at the Smithsonian, I couldn't shake it. Her name was New Jersey Skeleton 1972, but everyone called her Sandy: forever fifteen, presented to the museum's anthropology department by the police. A strange gift. I learned about her existence in a book published the year I was born about the epidemic of teen runaways between the late sixties and early seventies. My mother is the only grown-up teen runaway I know, but she was apparently a drop in a wave. New Jersey Skeleton 1972 was the phantom girl I was taught to fear becoming myself: the girl with the trusting smile, the girl with the grabbed wrist, the girl kept in the room, the girl dumped in a ditch.

Sandy had been spotted hitchhiking near the Jersey Shore in the spring of 1971, around the same time my mother left home the second time, for good. Six months later, two hunters discovered Sandy's body in a gravel pit on the side of US 30 near Egg Harbor, with nothing but a hotel key in the pocket of her flared denim trousers.

There was a man. Isn't there always? But he was cleared by the cops, deemed a good enough guy, though he was also old enough to book himself and Sandy into a motel and buy her the bell-bottoms she had on when she died. In *America's Runaways*, Christine Chapman reports what the man told the police: that she had said her name was Sandy, but he didn't believe her; and that she was on her way to Atlantic City to get a summer job with no bag, no nothing. He took care of her, bought her clothes, fed her, got them a motel room, and spent the night there. He went off to work in the morning, and when he came back two days later, she was gone. "He seemed kind, and she needed a place to stay," Chapman writes, though Sandy's bones could not corroborate this account. After waiting for her at the motel for two days—without calling the police—the man checked out and "returned to his routine and forgot about Sandy until New Jersey police confronted him with the fact of her death." For six months, he told no one about the girl who had vanished. Nobody tied a known missing person to the bones found in a roadside gravel pit. *He seemed kind.*

Six months after that, in 1972, the cops gave her body—a young and recent specimen, a rare prize for the anthropology department—to the Smithsonian, where they read her bones to see what story she might tell.

"Teenagers are an abstraction," a Smithsonian anthropologist told Chapman. "Until you know one, as I know Sandy, they are not very real to you."

But *did* she know Sandy? What could she know of her? Like Bruce Springsteen's Sandy, the South Jersey girl he pleads with in his song "4th of July, Asbury Park," she is a creation, a composite of every girl who took off from or toward something and ended up in a drawer, attached forever to some guy's story that frames him as the hero, the one who tried to save her and lost something of himself in the process. Imagine being left with only that. Could Madame Marie read this Sandy's fortune better than the cops could? What would she make of that man in the motel room? Of Sandy's parents, who never claimed her? Of the Smithsonian, that temple of knowledge?

Nine years after Sandy was found and donated to the museum, my mother, her long brown hair in braids pinned up on her head, pulled a cotton bikini from her dresser and folded it into a bag as my wail bounced off the wood floors of my parents' bedroom in our Jersey City apartment. The place smelled like incense and an aroma I would recognize much later as weed. She sat me down on the bed to explain that she was going down the shore for the weekend with her friends, and no, I couldn't come. She wanted a weekend away, that was all. She was twenty-three years old with a heartbreaker face, a weekend bag, and a red-faced preschooler racked with sobs on the bed. What she needed was a few days off to be herself, to not be anyone's mother. I was heaving and gulping. That she'd consider leaving me behind for a minute, let alone a whole weekend, was an outrage.

I watched her zip her bag, my little face a red mask of righteous fury. How old is a girl when her intuition arrives? Surely not this young. And yet maybe it's an evolutionary correction designed to give us a running start. Or it could be something we're born with that we spend years finding our way back to. I could not have known anything in that moment about what my mother had missed by leaving home at thirteen, getting married at fifteen, and having her first child before most girls her age finished high school, let alone what one weekend down the shore with childless young women her own age could have done to restore even just a part of that girl she had been when she first left home. I just knew I didn't want her to leave. I didn't want her to taste life without us.

I emailed the collection manager of archaeology and ethnology in the Smithsonian's Department of Anthropology to ask about Sandy. I wanted to see her. I couldn't quite articulate why in a way that didn't make me sound like a weirdo with a true crime podcast. Maybe I wanted to reassure her that someone remembered her, even if it was someone she had never met, someone who wasn't even alive when she had died. Maybe it was to confront the end I grew up fearing the most. This collection manager couldn't help me, but he referred me to one of the museum's forensic anthropologists. He also couldn't help, but he referred me to another anthropologist who had been at the museum when Sandy was admitted to the collection. That senior anthropologist had no recollection of this "specimen," as he called her, and he referred me back to the forensic anthropologist. The emails were polite but dizzying. How could a missing girl go missing again, decades later? The first time was a tragedy. Losing her again was a farce.

At my persistent request, the forensic anthropologist took a closer look at the records and discovered that Sandy had been "deaccessioned" from the collection.

"These are restricted files, so I will have to go to the National Anthropological Archives to look at this file and see what documentation is in this file," he told me. "If you want access to the file, you will have to get written permission (on letterhead) from the Atlantic Co. Medical Examiner's office."

When I looked for a contact there, I found yet another roadblock. The Atlantic County Medical Examiner's office had vanished—along with, presumably, its letterhead—the casualty of a bureaucratic merger. Once again, Sandy lay in limbo, unclaimed. I tried to deaccession her from this story, to put her out of my mind, but I couldn't.

The first time I realized I could disappear, I was at the Ringling Brothers and Barnum & Bailey Circus in Madison Square Garden with my preschool class from Mt. Pisgah, an African Methodist Episcopal church in our neighborhood. I was the only white child in the group, and as the family story goes, a police officer confronted my teacher, demanding she explain my presence. As if I had vanished from where I belonged and turned up here, a single blond kid swept up by Black strangers and therefore suspicious, even though I wasn't sad, I wasn't crying, and I was just enjoying the circus with my friends. I was a girl out of context for him because his rules for how to see a girl were rigid and underdeveloped. But I was exactly where I was supposed to be. My teacher and I both knew it, and she told him so.

The second time, I was at Sea World in Southern California, one in a series of theme park visits Mom took us on after we had moved from Jersey City to a town in Arizona within easy driving distance of San Diego. Everywhere I looked there was something new and interesting: orca puppets, carnival snacks, "This Way to the Sea Lions" signs. I was holding a hand and then wasn't. Something had caught my eye: a joyful pod of small stuffed dolphins cascading out of a display bin. At home I had Cristobel, the one-eyed plush kitten, a half-blinded victim of rough play; Gregory, the thrift-store stuffed pig; and fancy Madame Alexander baby dolls in impeccable pink frocks. But I did not have a small stuffed dolphin, and their chaotic clown smiles beckoned. When I turned my face up to catch my mother's eye and plead my case, she was gone, leaving a crowd swirling around me, every set of vacationing knees belonging to someone else's parent.

I was not sad; I was not crying. I felt a sense of calm come over me that even now, decades later, I still feel as soon as a crowd spills out around me and I know I could slip into it and let it carry me away. But a little kid alone in a crowd—even a silent, awestruck one—is easily spotted. She is untethered to permanence, a dandelion in the breeze. The question is only who gets to her first. In my case, a young woman—though possibly older than my mother was at the time, I realize now—knelt down to look me in the eye.

"Are you lost, honey?" she asked.

I didn't think I was lost. I thought I'd been left. There's a difference. But I took her hand, and she led me back to the lost-kids repository, which tried to be cheerful, soothing, distracting. There were toys, and I busied myself with a puzzle. Who knows how much time went by? I heard a voice describing me. It finished by saying, "She's only five years old."

"I'm SIX," I announced from the other room. My mother and I were reunited, and for the next several decades, she would tell the story about the time I ran away at Sea World, how one minute I was there and the next I wasn't, even though that isn't how it happened at all. I never moved; she did.

Maybe, on a cellular level, I understood something about my mother's capacity for wildness, her ability to morph into a new identity to save herself, to sense when the moment was right to wriggle away. After all, she had done it before, though I did not know that then. I don't know how old I was when I understood my mother was different from other mothers. It must have been a gradual awakening to the truth of her, pieced together from context clues and overheard adult conversations pockmarked with gaps nobody wanted to fill in. But to a small child, the most frightening thing imaginable is how easily a mother could slip into a different life, simple as a sundress she could stroll in down the boardwalk in a seaside town where nobody knows her. I may have been just a little kid, unable to fathom that there could be a party happening somewhere that didn't include me. But maybe there was another reason besides blunt umbrage that caused me to flip out at the idea of her going down the shore and leaving me behind. I was inconsolable, and she had a choice to make.

Ten minutes later, we were sitting side by side on our front stoop, a backpack for me next to her bag, waiting for Kathy to arrive. I did not yet have any way of appreciating how nimbly my mother could improvise and change course without admitting defeat. John and Daddy were still staying home. This was still going to be her girls' weekend, just like she'd planned. But I had made my case and secured my passage. I thought that she could be my big sister on this trip; she could pretend she was just babysitting me. I leaned against her as we waited for Kathy's car, pulling my sleeves over my curled fists and believing with all my tiny heart that I had just won a clean fight.

Eight of us crammed into that bungalow in Asbury Park—Mom, Kathy, my Uncle Russ's wife at the time, and a handful of Kathy's friends. It was a quintessential girls' weekend down the shore, the stuff of Springsteen songs: the boardwalk, the arcade, the beach. Beers for them and ice cream for me, the doted-on pet, the little sister of the weekend. Mom and I got a room to ourselves while the rest of the girls bunked up together. This was a test, I believed at the time, and we both passed: I had proven my devotion to her by refusing to let her out of my sight, and she had proven to me that even if she went to the literal end of the earth, she would take me with her.

There was a third time I realized I could disappear. The same year as the Sea World incident, I accompanied my mother's boyfriend on a day trip to Mexico. We lived in Yuma, Arizona, where we had moved to be near my mother's parents after she had left my father; he died a few later, back home in New Jersey. My mother's new boyfriend was a German soldier who was stationed at the Air Force base in Yuma like a military exchange student—blond, tan, straitlaced to the point of being uptight, and honest to a fault. He was the very opposite of my late father.

Yuma is a border town, and once, when he had some business on the other side while babysitting me, I went along. Boring adult stuff. Drowsy from the afternoon heat, I fell asleep in the back seat on the drive home. When he stopped at Customs and Border Protection on the way back from Mexico, the officer looked at the little girl asleep in the back, eyeballed the man with the foreign accent bringing her in from another country, and asked who she was. My mother's new boyfriend, though he did not lie as a rule, rolled the dice on simplicity and said I was his kid. This should have worked; my mother's boyfriend might have been a foreigner, but he was a white European foreigner, which I know now tends to enact the benefit of the doubt.

And here I must emphasize what a boring, routine day this was, babysitting for his girlfriend who was at work or running mundane errands. Today, he and my mother have been married for decades. He's my baby sister's father. He tried and failed to teach me how to drive and escorted my mother to both of my weddings. We are family.

But back then, a feeling I couldn't control flared inside my chest. From the back seat, I spoke up, because the truth in that moment felt like the only thing I owned.

"He's *not* my father!" I said.

I had committed a grave error, even if I couldn't understand the implications of the optics: a sleeping little girl ferried casually across international borders by a man whose right to do so was now being questioned. To the border patrol officer, everything was fine until I spoke up and made myself a problem they then had to work out.

I knew about stranger danger. Etan Patz's disappearance a few years earlier from his Manhattan neighborhood had rattled my mother, and she had drilled into our heads that we were never to speak to adults we didn't know, never to follow them anywhere. She knew how easy it was for a kid to disappear. But my mother's boyfriend wasn't a stranger. And yet he wasn't my father either. I couldn't tell you, or the officer, what we had even been doing in Mexico. Commotion ensued. I had done the wrong thing by contradicting his lie, which at the time I took as an outrageous provocation, an assault on what I knew was real and true. It's a fight I lost when this story became solidified as a piece of family lore, told to this day as *that time Erin almost got him arrested for human trafficking*, a hilarious tale in which I'm the punchline. This is another way a girl disappears, the time she first understands that her truth matters less than a man's comfort.

A question I return to again and again as I think about my mother and Sandy, the skeleton girl in the Smithsonian: What is the difference between a missing kid and a runaway?

When my mother left home, the dramatic increase in runaways since the mid-sixties was still largely treated by law enforcement as a nuisance to be contained and deterred. Do-gooders saw kids like her as a population of vulnerable individuals who needed constructive resources, but their mission was often at odds with a law-and-order establishment that treated vagrancy, truancy, and panhandling as just more evidence of baffling antisocial behavior by a generation of habitually wayward youth. Several years of media coverage of middle-class flower children, starting in 1967's Summer of Love, had created a one-dimensional portrait of the urban teen runaway as an undisciplined nonconformist in search of thrills, though coverage increasingly turned ominous as hard drugs and violence followed.

A 1968 profile in the *New York Times* of the late thirteen-year-old Deborah Neill was one such story. Four days after arriving to the city from Ohio, she was raped, and she had either been thrown from a fifth-floor window on Mott Street or had died trying to jump to her escape. The *Times* piece cast her as "one of the thousands of restless youngsters who flock to New York City from around the country hoping to find a new and freer life in Greenwich Village and the East Village, and who all too often find instead a life of violence, drugs and disillusionment." In another *Times* report about the 1971 indictment of thirteen men in the torture and rape of four runaway girls—"who came to New York seeking adventure"—as a prelude to being forced into prostitution, Bronx District Attorney Burton B. Roberts informally widened the indictment. "The indication is that runaway girls are fair game for people who would make a racket from it," he said. "If this is part of the youth culture, it is time we start exposing it for what it is and start eradicating it." Each girl was in danger once she didn't come home for dinner or report to homeroom or work the next day, no matter how or why she left in the first place. I see my mother in each of these girls, and in Sandy—the heartbreaking distance between what they sought and what found them.

In those days, the mechanisms for finding missing children were pretty lackluster. When two-year-old Elizabeth Gill—at that age, clearly a missing child, not a runaway—vanished from her own front yard in Cape Girardeau, Missouri, in 1965, the Center for Missing and Exploited Children was still almost twenty years away from being formed. Hers is the longest-running missing child case in the Show Me State. After little Beth disappeared, *Dateline* reported in 2019, her father wrote a letter to President Johnson, pleading with him to declare her case a likely kidnapping and open an FBI investigation; he based this on witnesses who had encountered a transient couple engaged in shady business and who had left town suddenly on the day Beth was last seen. J. Edgar Hoover responded, saying that although Beth had been logged in FBI files as a missing person, without evidence of a kidnapping, they couldn't investigate, though they would help local police follow up on any out-of-state leads. This level of police impotence seems surreal now in the age of the Amber Alert and viral social media posts, to those of us whose childhoods were shaped by John Walsh's Code Adam and the sheer stamina of TV newscasts when they covered stories of abducted girls. In terms of infrastructure, of official response and national coordination, it *was* a different time when Beth Gill disappeared. And a missing toddler is not, of course, the same as a missing teen. But it was not a different time in terms of our understanding of danger and safety, only of our bureaucracy. Cape Girardeau rallied around the Gill family and their missing daughter. Search parties formed. They dragged the Mississippi River because people have always known that a missing child is an endangered child, and that is true no matter the age of the child in question.

But public sympathy is frequently contingent on presumed innocence. A two-year-old has it. A thirteen-year-old might not. This disturbing reality remains true today as disappearances of pretty, young white women and girls often receive national media coverage and public support while missing Black, Indigenous, and other girls and women of color, as well as trans girls and women, often do not. Even within the protected class of pretty, young white women and girls, it must first be explicitly stated by a person with the authority to make it true—white parents of good community standing, generally speaking—that a good girl has vanished. Only then can the media and the authorities know how invested they should be in finding her and bringing her home.

A short five years after Beth Gill became a missing child, my mother was thirteen, with a brief history of behavior most would now consider to be little more than lightly rebellious. She was the middle child of a new family in town whose father was away at war. I can believe that police, if they were even enlisted to search in the first place, might have been less invested in her safe return than they would have been for the daughter of a more established local family. I can believe residents of that small town would not have stopped to think something was out of place if they saw my mother hitchhiking— so many kids did back then. But I can't square the grandmother I knew—imperious, persistent, not satisfied by platitudes or slipshod work—with the realization that she did not devote herself entirely to raising hell over her missing daughter. In the true crime version of my family's story, Grandmother should have never stopped demanding the police do their job and bring her home. In the true crime version of my family's story, my mother is not the suspect. There had been trouble at school, which she had alluded to at points throughout our childhood. Violence. And in the true crime version of this story, beleaguered detectives would have "looked at" the classmates who targeted her, only to come up empty-handed when their alibis checked out. The violence would only be a red herring if you were looking for a perpetrator, though, not a reason for her to leave on her own. This is not a true crime story—not that kind, anyway.

So. Why did my mother really leave home the first time? Not for the reasons I thought of as typical runaway triggers: abusive or addicted parents, her own drug or alcohol abuse, financial precarity, predatory grooming. Why do thirteen-year-olds do anything? Because their prefrontal cortex is still a dozen years away from being complete? Because it will piss someone off, and the ability to piss someone off is proof they exist? Do I really need an answer to this question now?

What is the difference between a runaway kid and a missing child?

Officially: a means, a reason, and agency to leave willingly, as opposed to a suspicion of foul play. In other words: a runaway is not a good girl.

Unofficially: a runaway kid is a missing child in search of a search party.

———————————

I found the right form to submit to the consolidated New Jersey Southern Regional Medical Examiner's Office, and I mailed my request for a letter of permission to view Sandy's files in the National Anthropological Archive, which I acknowledged was "a little odd." A medicolegal death investigator emailed me back. She couldn't release any information about Sandy to me because the case of her death, while cold, was still open. She gave me what she could: a missing persons number to look up in the national database and an offer to have a staff anthropologist run DNA or dental records of any missing person I might suspect could be Sandy against her records.

"Stay safe," she signed off.

I plugged Sandy's number into the database. There she was, in more detail than I thought possible. She was small: 5'3", 118 pounds. She dyed her hair, which was found in shades of blond, brown, and red brown. "Body discovered in woods off of Jim Leeds Road near milepost #42 of the Garden State Parkway in Galloway Township, New Jersey," it read. "All parts recovered; not recognizable—near or complete skeleton." She wore "a ribbed blue cotton or synthetic shirt"; "white, blue, and orange striped canvas or cotton trousers of the hip-hugger variety"; underwear and a white bra; and brown leather sandals—all found on her body. On her wrist, she wore a wide brown leather band inlaid with small brass grommets, a delicate ladies Westclock watch embedded in it—a perfect contradiction of girlish and rocker style.

And there was her face, or at least several artistic renderings of it, no two looking alike: a couple of scowling, crude police sketch composites from 1971 and '72; one 3D computer model in which she looked a bit like Mariel Hemingway the year she filmed *Manhattan*. One girl can be so many girls all at once. There was also one more recent portrait: home-trimmed bangs framing her alert eyes, her mouth almost ready to smile at a man's jokes.

I found myself feeling attached to Sandy, but I was just the latest person to fail her. I had no leads for the medicolegal death investigator's cold case, no DNA for the anthropologist to cross-reference against hers. I had nothing to give this girl. I wanted someone to know—the clothing store clerk, the motel manager, the diner waitress, the man who had bought her those striped hip-huggers and then forgotten about her until the police came calling—that a girl doesn't just vanish as if she never existed.

Where was Sandy going when she met the man who bought her new clothes, fed her at a diner, and then took her back to a motel? When did she decide to name herself Sandy, leaving her given name behind? If she had a little sister, had that sister ever visited the Smithsonian on a school field trip, or later as a parent taking her own kids, without even knowing whose secrets the anthropology department contained?

I thought about what she had told the man, who seemed kind, about her plan to go to Atlantic City and find work. In Springsteen's "Atlantic City," which I love for its Catholic embrace of redemption through sacrifice and resurrection, the protagonist attempts to explain to his girl why he's pinning his last hopes for the future on a desperate crime. The song is a mournful confession and, depending on how you hear it, possibly not entirely truthful. He has insurmountable debts, but he doesn't mention how they have been incurred. Resentful and bitter over his lot, he is willing to gamble on this path, which he knows is a cheat, and bring her along with him into the aftermath. All he asks of her is that she fix herself up nice and be there waiting after he does a favor that presumably will lead to the squaring of his debts. We don't know if the girl believed him or not, if she ripped up the ticket or pinned her hair up and put on her lipstick and went after her man. We don't get to know how she felt when he failed to show up, as this doomed man almost certainly did, at their boardwalk meeting spot. The song is not her story.

Sandy's bones couldn't tell me hers, either. A girl heads to the beach to trust her secrets to the tides, or she runs away from its switchblade lovers and carnival lights. Same mythical woods, different direction. While this Sandy slipped that motel key into her pocket, Bruce Springsteen wandered the Asbury Park boardwalk, carrying Madam Marie's mysteries of the future in his. Marie Castello, the boardwalk fortune-teller, lived to be ninety-three years old; Sandy never saw another set of fireworks over Little Eden. She couldn't have known that her chosen name would become synonymous with a young man's conflicted love for a home he could leave at any time to wander the earth unharmed, being reasonably sure he would be welcomed back when he decided it was time. A girl who steps out of order like that, the world so often shrugs, might deserve whatever happens as a result. Just as a young man on the road is stripped down to the essence of manhood in search of the clarity of purpose that freedom brings—with or without a woman strapped to his side—a runaway becomes an elemental girl, a symbol of everything illicit and seductive about youth and female sexuality, a ticking bomb, a crime scene in waiting.

In high school, when I was just a year older than Sandy was when she died, I memorized all two hundred and six bones in the human body. I learned how to name a skeleton part by part, from parietal to distal phalanx. It helped to carve the whole down into parts. I'd start with a small, manageable story: one hand has twenty-seven bones, split into three types—the carpals, the metacarpals, and the slippery phalanges. My practice skeleton was a body scribbled over, a story constantly revised and worn thin by eraser, a constellation of arrows surrounding each carpal by which she could be lured, dragged, pinned: trapezium, scaphoid, lunate, capitate. Rough jewels clustered like sea-tumbled shells, like gravel on a highway shoulder.

That was then; the answers were clear. Now, only tests I can't pass.

If you don't even know who your own mother is, what else don't you know?

Counterpoint: Can anyone ever know who their mother is? What mother would allow it?

I grew up understanding a basic outline of events. My mother vanished, left home at thirteen and didn't come back. After a few wild years in New York City, she married my father, had two kids, and moved to Jersey City, where she got her GED and went to nursing school to become an LPN. She returned to her parents' home across the country with us in tow when I was five, leaving my father back in New Jersey, where he died.

It turned out that was only half of it. My mother had lived another life, given herself another name I didn't know about until I began interviewing her about what had led her to date my father, how she had come to live in New York as a kid in the first place. She answered my questions for hours on the phone—some conversations are easier that way, I've learned—and I asked her to start at the beginning.

I learned my mother ran away twice. The first time, in 1970, she named herself Megan. She went home briefly but left again a few months later, in the spring of 1971, with a new name, Alexis, the one she kept. In between was a brief reprieve where she tried to be a good girl, tried junior high again, tried to fit in. In that interstitial period,

Megan disappeared from the family narrative. She became a secret only a handful of people knew about before now.

I thought I was writing a book that would help me understand my father's decision to marry a girl young enough to be his daughter and build a life with her. I didn't know that it would lead me to a ghost story.

What's the difference between a missing girl and a runaway? The world doesn't always want to hear how the runaway broke free. But I did. Megan was the missing piece all along. I wanted to know her in a way I could never know Sandy or any of the other girls whose stories I know only through the newspaper postmortems on their violent, tragic ends. And all I had to do, this whole time, was ask.

4
The Rules of Hitchhiking

In an upstairs bedroom of a red brick two-story home that used to be a boarding house, sprinting distance from the pretty white Gothic Revival house on the bluff overlooking the Missouri River where Amelia Earhart was born in Atchison, Kansas, my mother—who was not quite thirteen years old—tucked her curtain of straight brown hair behind her ear and sat down on the floor with a pile of magazines. She winced; the bruise on her thigh was still fresh. The new Jefferson Airplane record, *Volunteers*, had been on all afternoon, those riffs in "We Can Be Together" digging under her ribs like actual fingers, replacing the dull throb from a fist with something ferocious she couldn't quite yet name. This girl, too, felt like an outlaw. Grace Slick, with her kohl-rimmed eyes and thousand-yard stare, her icy cool on stage, was her idol, the kind of woman she wished she already was. Before her eighth-grade school year would start, this girl would disappear from this house with the white wraparound porch, from this small Kansas town with the pedestrian mall and the municipal swimming pool. She would walk right out of the frame with only the clothes on her back.

It was early January; the trees in her town were bare. The massacre at Kent State was still two months away. Here she was, cutting out a photo of a flower from an advertisement, carefully trimming around the curve of each petal. Glue in hand, she methodically affixed the flower in place on the plywood board. She'd been cutting out photos from magazines, saving images from ads, words and phrases from headlines: photos of soldiers marching, of kids dancing at Woodstock, of protesters facing the White House, holding up signs like "Silent Majority for Peace." Her father had returned to Vietnam at Christmas for his second tour, assigned to the Thirty-Fourth Supply and Services Battalion, running the Army Depot in Da Nang. This was personal to her.

She leaned back, considered the composition, and added a cutout of a building on fire. Almost done. She picked up her red marker and wrote, in bold looping strokes, around and between the images: *What If They Gave a War and Nobody Came?* She had sworn a vow of nonviolence and intended to honor it until her father came home. She would be like a monk, a conscientious objector to the wrongness of the war and the world. She would not raise her hand against any living thing. The bruise on her leg would not dissuade her. My mother had made a bargain with the universe: one girl's peace to balance a father's war. She would sacrifice her own safety for his, and in exchange for this, she had decided, he would be returned to her alive.

Grandfather had moved the family to his home state of Kansas in the summer of 1969. He was a few credits shy of a bachelor's degree in business administration, and he planned to finish his studies at St. Benedict's College up the street. Grandmother said he needed a nice home life—not an Army base—for his last few months before his next deployment. Grandfather grew up, as he was fond of saying, "on a dirt farm in Kansas," and Atchison, a five-hour drive east across the flat state from his hometown of Colby, with its river and trees and hills, was and was not like home. He had volunteered to deploy again. Volunteering was the path to advancement for families like theirs, two ambitious kids of working-class parents who had made themselves over into an officer in the Airborne Division and his lady, in tailored suits and hand-beaded dresses no less. Volunteering helped move him up, once he'd returned from Da Nang, to the Lt. Colonel rank he retired with. My mother was effectively the middle child (one brother, Randy, was born severely disabled, and he died in 1967 in Winfield State Hospital, where he had been institutionalized), sandwiched between the oldest boy, Ricky, and Rusty, a goofball two years her junior. They rented their old house. Room numbers were still nailed to each bedroom door. Her mother took a job at the college as the secretary to Father Timothy Fry, editor of the *American Benedictine Review*. The boys worked on the grounds crew at St. Benedict's Abbey under Brother Martin and made friends with boys in the neighborhood. And my mother? She had nowhere to be. She had nothing to do but stay out of trouble.

But she didn't know how to be the new kid in a public school, especially not in a small town full of civilians who had known each other since they'd been in diapers. Military kids are used to moving every six to eighteen months, and on base, everyone is the new kid all the time, so nobody ever feels out of place for too long. Army brats learn how to make fast and loose friendships with each other. You could be best buddies for months and then gone, sometimes without even a goodbye. Here, things were different. She did the things she was supposed to do in the small town's public school. She sang in the choir. She joined pep club to cheer on the football and basketball teams, with her mother sewing the uniform—a green corduroy vest and skirt she wore over a white blouse—to save money. Everyone was in the pep club. She could blend in there.

But there was wearing a handmade green corduroy vest to support the school and there was belonging, she learned. One day in the hallway, rushing to beat the bell between classes, she bumped shoulders with a girl we'll call Deborah.

Deborah said something smart. My mother said something back.

The next thing my mother knew, Deborah's fist connected with her head, her gut, her arm. She dropped her books in shock, then doubled over and took it. Then she felt herself being pulled up by her long, straight hair, Deborah's fist tangled through it, pinning her to the lockers with nowhere to go, her midsection exposed for more pummeling.

There is no more stubborn creature on Earth than a seventh-grade girl. My mother did not break her vow of nonviolence, not even to defend herself, not even when tested like this. She didn't raise her hand to another living creature, even one as furious and strong as the girl in front of her.

In the principal's office, he asked her what had happened.

"Deborah beat me up," my mother said. She wasn't a snitch, but everyone had seen. There was no other way to say it.

"Why did she do that?" he asked. "What did you do?"

"I didn't do anything," she said.

"That's just not possible," he told her. "You had to have done something."

She tried to collect herself.

"Behave yourself," the principal said, dismissing her.

Deborah was also back in the halls that day. But my mother had snitched. From then on, she felt she was marked. Some girls learned fast that they could hit the new kid and she wouldn't hit back. If the Colonel had been home, he might have coached her on how to punch back, as he did my brother when we were kids. If he had been home, maybe she would have fought. But a promise was a promise, even if she'd made it only to herself.

She tried to make herself invisible. Don't talk to anyone, don't bump into anyone. Face down, books to chest. Fade into the walls. But no matter how carefully she planned her route through the halls, she couldn't hide forever. One day, she turned a corner and saw Deborah standing in the middle of the hallway, backlit by the sunlight behind her. Not a single other soul in sight. They faced each other. A showdown.

Deborah charged, a train barreling down the tracks, and unleashed hell. Fists, feet, open palms, beating my mother down the hallway as she stumbled backward, trying in vain to shield herself from the blows without hitting back. They came to an open door. My mother remembers both of Deborah's palms square against her chest, then the air, the slow-motion flight in reverse, her hair streaming past her face, shielding her peripheral vision. Deborah's face was a mask of fury. Then, darkness.

The next thing my mother saw, flat on her back at the foot of the concrete stairs on the sidewalk outside the school, was her English teacher's concerned face.

"I must have tripped," my mother said, testing her jaw. She walked home alone, her gray skirt and gold satin blouse, a chic combo, torn and dirty.

"What happened to you? Were you hit by a car?" Grandmother asked when she walked in the door, aghast at her appearance.

"I got beat up."

There was no other way to say it. What she didn't say: "Make it stop." A mother is supposed to know that part.

But Grandmother did not pin up her blond hair in a French twist, put on her mod pearlescent lipstick and Mikimoto pearls, and walk down to the school and demand to see the principal. She did not call the other girl's parents to try to broker a truce.

Maybe it was hard enough getting up every day and going to Father Timothy's office like her husband wasn't away at war, hard enough plating up family dinners while news anchors reported yet another round of casualties coming home. She was calmer during this deployment than during his first tour in 1966 and '67. She didn't explode at the kids over nothing, over the normal kid stuff they couldn't really help. But at any moment, she could have slipped back into a depression, started painting bleak portraits like she had the last time. Maybe she had made her own bargain with the universe to bring her husband home alive.

Or maybe Grandmother just thought it wasn't serious and the moment would pass. That the fighting would stop on its own so she wouldn't have to walk into a strange school's office without her husband's rank to back her and demand some civilian man in an inadequate suit take her seriously. Grandmother knew her charm to be a weapon. She also knew when it was insufficient for the job.

The school didn't call her either. The other kids looked away when it happened. My mother was sent to study hall twice as punishment for being such an easy target. When the school year ended, it was a relief. She hadn't decided yet that she wouldn't be going back.

———————————

That was the year my mother didn't come home when she was supposed to for the first time. When she finally sneaked in past midnight, after drinking a little too much, Grandmother lost her mind. "Where have you been?" *Smack.* "I called Paula's father." *Smack.* "Two o'clock in the morning." *Smack.* "You were supposed to be at the movies!" My mother says now that she deserved it. She knew she had crossed a line.

But the lesson didn't stick. The second time my mother didn't come home, she stayed out longer. She knew a girl whose brother-in-law owned an empty house across town. It wasn't far, but it was as far as my mother had ever been on her own. She was used to traveling light—for each move the Army dictated, Grandmother gave each of her children just one box for their toys and anything other than clothes and necessities. My mother packed a bag, tucked in some photographs and a few outfits. But someone noticed and made a phone call. She was on her own for five blissful hours until Grandmother pulled up outside the house and dragged her home.

"Are you out of your goddamned mind?" Grandmother demanded. "You don't know what kind of people are out there."

In comedy, the rule of three describes a pattern of rapid repetition that builds tension the third delivery subverts, causing cathartic release. A tragedy on stage is delivered in three acts. In fairy tales, the third incantation binds or breaks the spell. For my mother, one late summer day in 1970, the phone rang. On the other end was a boy she had met on a family vacation in Colorado a month earlier. They'd had a brief summer romance, the stuff of adolescent crushes and kissing after ice cream. He was not yet old enough to drive himself to Kansas to visit her. When he asked if she'd like to go back to Colorado, she shrugged and said, "Sure, when?"

"Meet me downtown in thirty minutes," he said.

This kid had hitchhiked out of Colorado and across the entire length of Kansas to ask my mother out on a date. It was a grand gesture, the exact right move to win over a girl like her. "I knew you weren't happy here," he told her on the phone, and it felt like for the first time, someone had been listening.

This time, she didn't stop to pack a bag. She took no mementos or changes of clothes. She grabbed her jean jacket, her purse—contents: a nondescript kid's watch, a hairbrush, lip gloss, and less than a dollar in change—laced up her sneakers, and said she was going for a walk by the river. Maybe she didn't think they'd really get very far, or maybe she didn't think much about what would happen next at all. But in that moment, an escape hatch presented itself and she slipped through it. She walked out of the house, turned the corner, and within minutes, she and the boy were on the side of the road with their thumbs outstretched.

This is how a girl vanishes, without even a folding bill to her name.

———————————

It took my mother two days with her thumb out on the interstate to cover the 620 miles between Atchison, Kansas, and Evergreen, Colorado. She and the boy slept on park benches when they could because the second rule of hitchhiking is never fall asleep in someone else's car. The first rule is never get into the back seat of a two-door car. The third rule is never believe a word the driver says. She never believed the drivers anyway; everything she said back to them was a lie. If everyone was a liar, nobody was breaking the rules.

It wasn't easy for two people to get picked up, but it was easier for a boy to hitchhike with a girl—she made him seem less dangerous. If my mother saw a VW van with a peace sign on its hood, she knew they were in good company. Freaks would feed them; they'd let the boy smoke. Farmers too were good and plentiful, loading both kids into the front bench seats of their field-scarred trucks and dropping them in the next town. It was the square adults, middle-class in their late-model sedans, who would do things like slow down and pull over to the shoulder with their brake lights on and wait as the kids ran to catch up and then, just as they got close, peel off, leaving them out of breath and feeling foolish. They managed to avoid being spotted by cops, which was lucky. She figured the boy might tell the truth if questioned. She had already decided that wasn't an option.

They rolled into Evergreen, Colorado, in midmorning. They walked up to a clearing overlooking the town, a picnic spot with tables and a nice view. Wait here, he told her.

"I've been gone for a few days. I've got to go home for a bit," he said. "I'll be right back."

She sat at the table and waited. And waited and waited. Squirrels frolicked up the trunks and around the roots of the trees. Birds sang in a place where nobody knew she wasn't supposed to be. She sat and enjoyed the busyness of nature and the absence of people. What would they do with their day when he came back? What would happen tomorrow? There was no plan, which suited her just fine.

The sun rose high in the sky and then dipped down and began to fade slowly behind the mountains. The boy didn't return. It would be dark soon, and darkness meant animals—bobcats, bears, whatever else lurked up in the hills. Even a stubborn girl has to admit when she's been stood up. She could try to find a phone, call home, and ask her mother to come get her. But she remembered her mother's anger the time she had blown curfew, the way her mother's mouth had grown larger and larger, morphing into a cartoon black hole as she yelled about safety and responsibility and the ditch my mother could have been dead in. That was for slinking home past midnight; this was two whole days on the road and getting discarded like an old toy on a mountain trail.

She heard an engine roar in the distance. She walked across the clearing and peered down to see a motorcycle driving up the road. A man got off and wandered away, maybe to pee. A motorcycle, she thought. That's an idea.

Car doors lock, but a motorcycle leaves you in the open air. Someone can hear you scream. As she saw it, only one option held any possibility of a positive outcome: keep moving.

When the man reemerged from the woods, she was standing next to his bike. He was tall, older—in his mid-twenties, maybe—with blue eyes and long curly blond hair that almost glowed in the magic-hour light.

"Hey," she said, acting casual, like she'd just been looking for him this whole time. "What're you doing?"

Let's call this young man James. He was headed to Aspen, he said. Did she want to go?

"I'm Megan," she said, getting on the back of his bike. "My parents kicked me out of the house when I turned eighteen, so I've just been traveling around."

That was her first lie, naming herself. More lies came just as easily. Once she shrugged off her real name and age and family, she was no longer just a girl who had broken curfew in a disastrous and thorough way. As far as anyone knew now, she was Megan Shane, legally responsible for herself. She could go anywhere she wanted to, be from where she wanted, and nobody could say a word. She could see any part of the world she wanted to, taking from it what it would give.

As night fell, James drove Megan toward Denver. Rather than head for the city, he took her up a series of closed roads, maneuvering the bike around barricades to the top of a high hill, where the city lights glittered below them like diamonds spread out on a rug. He unrolled a sleeping bag and started to build a fire. They would camp there for the night, then head to Aspen in the morning. This was an experience Megan could have. What else could Megan have if she decided she wanted it?

Maybe James thought the same thing. They kissed, and things went pretty far until he stopped short. When he began to suspect she was a virgin, it might have been the first time he really looked at her, and he pulled back, confused and a little dismayed.

"You've lied about a lot of stuff, haven't you?"

It wasn't really a question.

"Only some of it," she said.

"Okay," he sighed.

He turned away from her and fell asleep. Megan spent her third night away from home, not knowing if she'd be left alone on another hillside come morning.

My mother once accused me in high school of being willing to "trust anyone with purple hair," a metonym for what passed as counterculture in the early nineties in our small Kentucky town. Inside, I raged at the injustice of being called dumb without proof, wondering how she couldn't know her own daughter well enough to know that I didn't follow any guy with a good haircut wherever he wanted to go and that I was, in fact, a fairly cautious kid, skeptical even, someone highly invested in being perceived as too smart for all that, whatever *that* might have been. I had been raised by a streetwise mother who had survived the Lower East Side of the 1970s. But that was the eagle-eyed hard-ass who had taught me never to leave a door unlocked for a minute, not this girl who had climbed onto the back of a motorcycle driven by a man she had just met after hitchhiking her way ten hours from home with a boy she barely knew. I didn't know that girl. The Smithsonian anthropologist's words rang in my head: *Teenagers are an abstraction. Until you know one, they are not very real to you.*

The miracle of that night overlooking Denver wasn't that Megan found a ride but that she found it with a decent man, one who saw a girl on the road by herself as a vulnerable person and not a prize for him to claim. Out of context, as she was, a girl has no status, and therefore no presumed innocence in the eyes of the world.

"Behave and the world will behave accordingly" is a lie girls are taught from birth. It's a powerful one, and it presumes a girl can control how she is treated. Any girl can be seen as a potential runaway, one step from becoming uncontrollable, needing to be rescued from and punished for the freedoms she might claim. I can see now that this was the lesson my mother was trying to shield me from when she grounded me for blowing curfew by half an hour because my friend's mother was late picking us up from the mall, a small injustice I have nursed for decades as only a daughter could. She didn't trust me to make shrewd decisions, but not because I wasn't trustworthy or smart. At the end of the day, even a mother's baseless accusations reveal only the truth about the accuser, not the accused. She was trying to tell me something painful about herself.

———————

The morning after my mother's first night as Megan, she and James broke camp and rode down the hill toward Aspen. The Colorado resort town had only finished paving its downtown streets seven years earlier, and by the summer of 1970, the influx of hippies from all over the country who flowed in at the end of the sixties had mixed with the ski bums and the mountain old-timers to make a community unlike any other. It was a bustling sporting destination with a capacity of more than 26,000 skiers per hour in peak season and a full-swing counterculture in the summer.

James pulled his bike over on Main Street.

"This is where I leave you," he said to Megan. "You probably need to go home."

She probably did. But she thanked him for the ride and for taking care of her. Then she turned right and walked straight into Eden.

Aspen was just the place for a girl with long hair and no baggage to disappear into the crowd. Young people hung around without much apparent purpose except to be together, bringing drugs and music and a loose, accommodating energy. A sign on Main Street labeled "THUMBING STATION," featuring a bold outstretched hitchhiker's thumb, remains an icon and a landmark, a physical marker of the town's history as a way station for free spirits.

Megan turned down Cooper Avenue and walked into Wagner Park's throngs of young people—shirtless boys in suede vests and sunglasses, girls in wide-brimmed hats and flowing peasant blouses. She slid right into a game of Frisbee, and nobody acted anything less than pleased to have a new girl in their midst.

After they tired of Frisbee, a couple asked if she wanted to get high.

"Sure," she said.

It would be her first time, but she acted cool, following them to their Jeep and climbing into the back seat. The girl dug around in the glove compartment while the boy turned the key in the ignition and turned on the radio. A DJ's voice faded out, and suddenly, there were Ginger Baker's drumsticks clicking and Eric Clapton's baritone and Jeff Bruce's tenor hum floating above it. When the girl in the front seat finished rolling the joint, she lit it, took a hit, and passed it to the boy, who then passed it to Megan. The rolling papers were printed with the stars and stripes of the American flag, and it all seemed too perfect. She got high for the first time to Clapton's guitar wailing, all three of them screaming along to "I Feel Free." If this was Megan's life, she'd take it.

An older girl might have worried about being broke and having to survive, but Megan was just young enough to expect things to work out. And in Aspen, for her, they did. She experienced the community's vibe as strong yet flexible, like a reed that could bend in whatever direction the wind blew without breaking. Food and shelter, like the loaves and fishes Jesus multiplied, seemed to appear to fit the need. A burger in a restaurant could cost as much as a whopping six dollars, but that didn't matter; someone always had something extra to eat—granola was especially plentiful, so she practically lived on odd handfuls from communal twenty-pound containers. There was always a place to crash, and crashers like her—friendly, respectful, no sticky fingers—were welcome. One night, someone's couch wasn't spoken for, and she was welcome to it. Another night, there was room on the floor of an apartment where the party kept going until it didn't make sense to leave anyway. Someone always had a spare sleeping bag in their tent, an extra bunk on their converted school bus or on the floor in the back of their cheerful Westfalia camper with a tapestry on the wall. In this way, Aspen's social scene was oddly comfortable for a military brat—everyone was from somewhere else, nobody expected you to stay forever, and most people were happy to make friends immediately and only for as long as you were there.

The weather was kind in late summer, so being outside most of the day worked out. When she noticed herself getting ripe, she'd walk to the Roaring Fork River, take her clothes off, wash them and herself, put her wet clothes back on, and let them dry on her back in the sun. A fresh T-shirt and a spare pair of jeans came her way. A backpack, too, and a copy of an anthology titled *Twelve Poets*. She treasured that book, its brown cover now lined and cracked like sun-worn skin, from which she read us T. S. Eliot poems when we were young: "Macavity the Mystery Cat," of course, but also "The Hollow Men," which she knew by heart. Someone was always leaving something behind when they left. Everyone was generous, everyone had time, and no one asked too many questions. This radical hospitality took care of her when she needed it, and she has repaid it throughout her lifetime: an extra place setting at Christmas dinner for friends who had no family nearby, hand-me-down furniture and clothes for the woman who had fled her marriage with her kids and little else. I've inherited this tendency from her, to always want to give away a thing I no longer need to someone who does, to put an item out on the curb for the taking rather than listing it for sale, believing that these accounts always balance over time.

In Aspen, sex was recreation. It was community, a thing you could do even when you were broke. And it eluded Megan at first. Her lack of sexual experience was getting to be a problem, she thought, a mental and physical block in her campaign to literally make love, not war. Megan claimed she was eighteen, after all, a young woman out on her own, not some little girl heading into eighth grade. And yet there she was, still carrying her virginity around like a low-grade headache she couldn't shake. So she trained her eye on a cute guy who wore harmonicas tucked into bandoliers crisscrossed on his chest. It was a mildly disappointing experience. This was what everyone was always talking about?

Then smoldering Peter showed up. She thought he looked Spanish with his dark hair and dark eyes. He was a little older than her—maybe seventeen or eighteen, and he was just having a fun freak summer like so many others. He was going camping up in the mountains that week. Did she want to come? He had a backpack and a sleeping bag, food and water. They hitched a ride up the mountain and then walked about five miles into the forest to a pine lean-to next to a creek. They stayed in the woods for five days, and by the time she came down out of the forest, she knew what the first guy didn't.

Megan wasn't the only young girl experiencing Aspen that summer. Betsy, a fifteen-year-old from Boston, had been flown west by her parents to work for the summer at a ski lodge owned by family friends. They thought the mountains would be a more wholesome environment than Boston's tumultuous student protest scene, where Betsy had taken to running a bit wild. Her parents were likely not alone in being perpetually three steps behind their children, baffled by the rapid pace of cultural change, bereft of the tools they needed to deal with their suddenly crazy kids, and full of rage over their inexplicable rebellion.

Betsy's memories of Aspen are a little darker than my mother's. It was a time of incredible idealism, sure, but it was also mixed with a sort of hypocrisy about who peace and love were really meant for, which created conditions where saying no to men would get a girl labeled "uptight," a cardinal sin of the times.

Betsy took a photography course that summer with Nicholas Nixon at the Center for the Eye, where visiting faculty in that era included Henri Cartier-Bresson, Minor White, and Larry Clark. She met a staff photographer from a major metropolitan daily newspaper that summer, too, and he and Betsy went out for a while. She's pretty sure she still had her braces on.

The lodge owners didn't really keep up with her like parents might have, so even though Betsy's job kept her occupied during the day, once she was finished cleaning rooms, her time was her own. Mostly, she went to listen to music in the park, which is where she and Megan—elfin, wide-eyed Megan, she remembers—probably met, though neither can remember now. Sometimes when Megan needed a place to crash, Betsy would let her stay in the lodge's staff quarters with her. Betsy tried LSD for the first and last time in Aspen; someone stole the traveler's checks her parents had given her for spending money. Because her job only covered room and board, she joined the panhandlers in town for a while but ended up going back to Boston early.

In September, the days started growing shorter and cooler. The possibility of staying in Aspen forever dwindled. Little by little, after Betsy left, the scene in the park began to fade. School was starting, and the draft and its student deferment were still in place. Megan realized it was time to weigh her options. Should she keep her new life going on the road or call her mother and ask for help getting home? Nothing was keeping her in Aspen, but she had gotten a full taste of life as Megan, and she couldn't conceive of going back now.

A boy she knew from the park told her he was hitchhiking back East. She knew the rules; teaming up was safer than trying to do it on her own. Betsy had given her a phone number and address and had told her to look her up if she was ever on the East Coast.

"Let's go," she said. "I have a friend in Boston."

They stuck out their thumbs. Soon enough, a car pulled over. A familiar routine began.

"This is my old lady," the boy told the couple.

"He's my old man," Megan agreed.

They got in, and they were on their way.

Aspen was full of lost boys on an endless summer break, sunning stoned in the park like the happy dogs that roamed the streets of town. In Boston, Megan found men.

But first, hitching the final leg solo to her friend's suburban home in Wayland, she found Betsy. The family set up a cot for Megan in Betsy's room, and her parents eyed this new character in their daughter's life across the dinner table with resignation. Perhaps Betsy's parents were simply exhausted at that point. Her psychiatrist father dealt professionally with runaways, troubled kids, and the court system. It seems inconceivable to me that he would have believed thirteen-year-old Megan was really eighteen as she claimed. But if he tried to figure out where this girl with only a backpack and a vague story belonged, and to whom, he didn't try very hard. She was a runaway, not a missing child. And runaways belong to nobody.

Kids then must have been baffling to their parents who had grown up in the shadow of war; even those who were fortunate enough to have peace and prosperity at home didn't always seem to want it. Aspen became one of their playgrounds. Boston, as always, provided a crucible, an open laboratory of corners, commons, and campuses where experiments could play out.

Boston excited Megan more than the comfortable suburbs, and when Betsy's mother said it was probably time for her little friend to leave, Megan didn't hesitate. She went straight to Cambridge Common, where George Washington is said to have taken command of the Revolutionary troops, and, just like Aspen, she found a park scene to slip into: guys with guitars strumming in tight, furious circles, Hare Krishna kids chanting and drumming, their loose robes swirling in the autumn sun.

In Aspen, everything was expensive, and everything was free. Food, clothes, wine, weed, and a place to sleep just appeared for Megan and she accepted it all. Boston was different. She had to ask.

"Hey, I don't mean to bother you," she'd say, approaching a suburban shopper visiting Harvard Square, her wide green eyes and direct smile perfected by years of military moves, her straight posture and crisp diction shaped by parents who had taught her not to mumble, "but can you spare a quarter?"

If she didn't ask for much, people were willing to give. If enough people gave, she could afford a burger for dinner, something to drink.

There was a system, informal but effective: one kid wouldn't infringe on another's spot. So Megan had her post, and another girl we'll call Trina, sweet and friendly with curly brown hair, had hers.

A corner didn't belong to you, but you could belong to it. In Boston, kids were always running from something—school, the military, parents—so it was normal for someone to be there one day and gone the next, like when Trina didn't show up to her normal spot, Trina who had mastered the art of never letting a worry darken her eyes because that's what the scene wanted. Worrying meant you didn't trust the world to be good to you if you opened your heart and your eyes to it, and wasn't that what they were trying to prove?

Boston was saturated with kids like them. It was estimated there were anywhere from two to four thousand itinerant youth, a mix of minors and college dropouts, living in Cambridge at that time. They had flocked there, as they had to Haight-Ashbury and Greenwich Village, to form, as the *New York Times* described it, loose communities "forged from the improbable ingredients of idealism and alienation, radical politics and passivism, willful poverty, despair and massive amounts of hallucinogens." In another year or two, the hottest scenes around campuses and in city centers would be considered more or less dead, as the kids with resources returned to school or moved out to rural and suburban communes, leaving mostly lower-income, unhoused youth behind. A 1972 story about the Haight illustrated this shift, with some locals celebrating the neighborhood's transition into a kind of cautious stability as it emerged from the erratic violence of the hard drug scene that had followed the hippie golden years. But Boston's street scene in 1970 was still humming with kids. They slept in hostels and crash pads and at Sanctuary—in by nightfall, out by morning. A group of nuns drove a van around with doctors from Mass General, treating infections and fevers and offering sandwiches, psych referrals, or directions to a bed if you needed one.

When Trina came back to her corner, she had only been gone a week or two, but she looked different. These were the years before milk carton kids, before the stranger danger mantra. Trina disappeared to

New York, and when she came back, she was hurt really bad. In the Common, she and Megan passed the Process Church kids, Satanists dressed all in black; some kids were saying they were connected to the Manson murders (they weren't). Megan asked her what had happened, and Trina lowered her jeans. Bruises like wet leaves trailed up from her knees.

Trina said the name of a motorcycle club; she had met some bikers at their hang-out.

The medical van circled the block.

Megan remembered the feel of Trina's fingers working tenderly through her hair, crafting it into a crown of intricate braids, at the hostel where they stayed together. Trina had disappeared for a week or two, gone to New York, and come back like this, different. In Aspen, everything Megan needed came to her. Here, everything had a price.

In Boston, a man was also a roof, a bed, a table, a routine. Megan met a young man we'll call Tommy in Cambridge Common, went home with him, and stayed for a few days, a week—it was hard to say. Tommy lived in a building with windows that slid open like silent, expensive patio doors to reveal a view of MIT's Great Dome gleaming across the river. Tommy wasn't old, but he wasn't young. He was small enough that a skinny, barefoot girl like Megan could wear his clothes, and she did: his suede pants, his black velvet cape. In Aspen, you could look like a grubby camper; in the city, you wanted to have a look. Tommy had the best of everything as far as she could tell—food, booze, stereo, art, pants, cape, and a scarlet macaw that crouched on the table, watching her with unknowable eyes. Her mother had taught her to appreciate fine things but never to pay full price herself. Tommy had plenty to appreciate.

When she opened one of Tommy's expensive windows one day and knocked over a piece of artwork propped on the sill, it fell all the way down to the street, where it broke on a car.

"You can't be doing that shit," he scolded. He was nicer to the bird when it acted up, she thought. She had folded herself into his apartment, his life, but hadn't learned how to make herself seamless, a part of the decor.

"I wanted some air," she said. She looked at him. The macaw looked at her. She wrapped herself in the cape, walked out, and never went back.

I imagine how many neighbors must have seen her go in and out of Tommy's beautiful building with the view of MIT's dome, never asking this barefoot girl what size shoes she wore.

Word on Boston Common was that a room was opening up in a house in Cambridge. My mother, who had been crashing here and there after leaving Tommy's place—in hostels or with men or wherever she could find a friendly place for the night—met up with the housemates to ask about stepping in. They made a handshake deal with a thirteen-year-old who introduced herself as Megan, and nobody asked or cared if she really was as old as she pretended to be. Her room, the first of her own on her own, was barely a cupboard really, tucked beneath the staircase of a rambling Victorian shared by half a dozen students. It came furnished with a mattress and an empty dresser. The house had a revolving door of guests, university kids with money who did more extravagant drugs. Here, she met kids like a college freshman we'll call Gabe. He had a sweet, carefree smile, a head of dark curls, and he could do a dead-on impression of Joe Cocker's Woodstock performance of "With a Little Help from

My Friends." She cooked and cleaned for her housemates and did odd jobs, like picking pods out of a load of peyote buttons someone had hauled in from out West, to help pay her way.

One day in mid-September—it was still warm enough to go without shoes—she wandered with a kid called Chip to the top floor of the three-family house he was staying in to smoke a joint. Megan knew Chip from around the protest and music scene. He was another young kid, skinny with a mop of dirty blond, curly hair. Chip was hungry, and the kitchen in the house was empty.

"There's a store I can go to," Chip said.

"You got money?" Megan said.

"Hell no," he replied matter-of-factly. "But let's go get something to eat."

They walked to a small market, a little mom-and-pop joint with maybe two cashiers, the front display windows lined with bottles and cans. She parted from Chip at the door and wandered the aisles. The shelves groaned with packaged abundance: cans of Campbell's Golden Mushroom Soup and Betty Crocker Chocolate Pudding, boxes of Carnation Instant Breakfast and Chicken in a Biskit, new delicacies like Hamburger Helper and Orville Redenbacher's Gourmet Popping Corn. At the deli case, Chip shoved a package of hot dogs down his pants. He turned to walk back toward the front doors, and she followed. The clerk, who may have been watching them as soon as they walked in, who had maybe seen Chip steal from them before, beat them to it. As he turned the key in the lock, he said, "I've called the cops."

Megan had never stolen anything except a cape from Tommy, and to her, even that was more like a long-term loan; he could have it back any time he asked. Still, the clerk kept them both until the cops arrived.

"What happens now?" Megan asked Chip. They sat in the back of the car while the cop took down the clerk's report.

"I'm going back to foster care," he said. "They'll call your parents and send you home."

"That can't happen," she said. "My mother will have a coronary. My dad's in Vietnam."

"Yeah, it will," Chip said. "It happens every time."

Chip wasn't a lawyer, just a kid who had run away from a foster home. But he wasn't wrong about his or Megan's precarious legal status. At the time, the laws regarding the "unemancipated runaway child" were "both confused and confusing," according to a 1975 report from the Department of Health, Education, and Welfare, which made no bones about how "the law is more of a hindrance than a help to such a child." In nearly half the states at the time, the police had the right to take a suspected runaway child into custody, and since the late sixties, such arrests had been on the rise. They would peak in 1971 at more than 200,000 arrests of minors suspected of being runaways. Massachusetts was one state that policed such "status offenses"—actions that were criminalized based solely on the offender's status. You could be arrested for sitting on a park bench, talking to a friend. That is to say, simply existing was a potential crime if you looked younger than eighteen and couldn't prove your parents knew where you had been for the last forty-eight hours. To break a law on top of that—even if it was just standing by in a store while some kid you knew stuffed hot dogs down his pants—meant the possibility of being charged with an act of juvenile delinquency too.

Megan was arrested and charged with the status offense of being a runaway. She gave her name as Megan Shane and claimed she was twenty-two. With a skeptical look, the officer wrote down her birth date to make her seventeen. She was held with the women in Beacon Hill's Charles Street Jail, an imposing Boston Granite-style fortress with four wings that branched off its central rotunda like a cross. Protesting suffragists and notorious mobsters alike had stayed there.

Periodically, an officer would wander back to her holding cell, look at her for a moment, study a photo, then look at her again before walking away. She felt sure that soon enough, the photo in the officer's hand would be her seventh-grade yearbook picture and that the next day, her mother would be picking out the right dress to wear to collect her only daughter from a Boston jail.

An older woman we'll call Yvette, who had been a foster mother—she told Megan she'd stabbed her husband for beating one of the kids—took her under her wing.

"In jail, all the girls want to be your friend," she told Megan. "Stay away from them. They're bad girls. You stay by me, and nothing will happen to you."

Jimi Hendrix died a few days after Megan came to Charles Street, and his death hit her hard. She knew every note he played of "The Star-Spangled Banner" at Woodstock. That was the America she believed in. Megan tore the story about his death out of the newspaper that had been passed around and kept it tucked inside her wallet for almost twenty years, until the newsprint finally frayed at the ghost-soft folds.

To Yvette, who stayed true to her word, Megan was one of the good girls. But to the officers of the municipal court, Megan was just a liar and a pain in the ass. She went to court three times in a yellow polyester dress they made her wear, along with a pair of sensible shoes that made her feel like a nun. At a hearing on September 23, Judge Costello ran out of patience; he was not buying her story, and he didn't care that she hadn't stolen anything. He demanded to know who she was and where she was from. She needed to go home. All these kids needed to go home and straighten out if they wanted to have any future, harumph. But she couldn't fathom that. And when had being honest with a man behind a desk ever made her safe? So she doubled down in front of the judge: she was Megan Shane, she was twenty-two years old, her parents had kicked her out of their house, and she had no home address.

The Commonwealth of Massachusetts couldn't prove Megan was a minor, but she couldn't prove she wasn't. What is presumed innocence for a girl in America? It was determined, under the guise of enforced protection, that she needed to be punished for her status. They were going to keep her safe by locking her up. If she wanted the state's help getting home, she would have to ask.

"Young lady," she remembers the judge saying to her, "I don't believe you. You're a kid. I don't know how old you are, but you are much younger than you say."

He remanded her to a youth facility until she turned eighteen. Harsh, but not unprecedented. As a protective and preventative measure, girls were more likely to be detained for status offenses to begin with. America has never seen idle, wandering girls and boys in the same light. A boy naturally gains experience on the road, while a girl is assumed to suffer or weather damage. Perhaps the judge thought that the prospect of being in state custody until Megan became a legal adult would prompt her to give in and call home. He didn't know about her vow, about the girls in the hallways and on the sidewalks of Atchison. He didn't know anything about her and what she could take. Five years? So be it.

An officer drove her to the facility, told her to sit down in a chair, and left. In the intake administrator's office, she sized the older woman up and decided this wasn't the time to act tough. She buried her face in her hands and started to tremble.

"They beat me up in jail," she told the woman, raising her head to let her see the tears forming in her eyes. Maybe they were a genuine physiological response to the stress of jail, of court, of having what felt like the rest of her life decided for her just as she was starting it. Maybe they were just a manipulation, part of her act. Who's to say?

"I'm starving," she told the woman. "They never fed me."

The woman looked at this skinny mess of a girl. Everyone looks younger, more helpless, when they cry. None of what she said was true; thanks to Yvette, jail had not been dangerous for her. It was only frightening because of the possibility of being found out. Megan's bravado hadn't convinced the judge or the cops, but she was genuinely skinny and pathetic enough in that moment, perhaps, to sell her story. Her pitiful charm worked.

"I'm going to get you something to eat," she told Megan. "I'll be right back."

Is audacity learned or is it innate, like double-jointed fingers or the ability to roll your tongue? I won't move to an empty seat at a concert for a better view out of fear of being caught and reprimanded. I have a pathological fear of asking for forgiveness rather than permission. I grew up watching my mother haggle with vendors at flea markets and bargain down prices at yard sales with a cheerful efficiency that suggests she might even be doing the seller a favor by paying a lower price, but I would rather eat glass than inquire about the cost of something, let alone suggest that *less* would be better. At thirteen, I would have felt awkward walking into a store by myself, certain that everyone there was looking at me, waiting for me to do something stupid so they could laugh and point. I got the hall pass and did the homework. I was so sure that if I completed all the right steps in the right order, I would have nothing to forgive and would be granted all the permission in the world for whatever I wanted.

Megan listened to the woman's footsteps fade down the hallway. She stood up and peered out the door. The hall was empty. She stepped out of the office as softly as her nun shoes would allow and padded down the hallway. Nobody appeared to ask her where she was supposed to be and where she thought she was going. She opened the front door, slipped out, and closed it with a quiet click behind her.

Then she walked down the front steps, turned onto the sidewalk, pointed herself toward Boston Common, and melted into the crowd.

———————————

Running away from home was common in 1970; running away from juvie made Megan a minor celebrity among her peers gathered in the Common. *You did what?* They thrilled at her daring. *Like a jailbreak? What do you need? What can we help with?* She needed out of her court-ordered church dress and nun shoes, for starters. The little hippie mice and birds flitted around with their fairy-tale magic. A T-shirt and jeans and a pair of sneakers appeared to turn her back into Megan. She celebrated by picking the cutest boy out of the group to claim as hers, at least for the day.

October turned the leaves on her street orange and red and yellow. Janis Joplin died. Together with Jimi it was almost too much. A few weeks later, Megan ran into a guy she had scored acid from on occasion. Let's call him Greg. Did she want to go on an adventure with him? A bag of mescaline, a hotel room, a rendezvous he had in the lobby downstairs. She had no role except to accompany him; the rush of a big deal could be more fun with a pretty girl by your side, and her presence would be disarming. A guy wasn't likely to bring trouble if he brought his girl with him, the logic went, and if Greg had meant for her to be camouflage for a rip-off rather than a sign of good intent, she wasn't aware of it. They hitchhiked to a hotel near the airport, and he checked them into a room. They hid the mescaline inside the fire extinguisher case in the hallway, and he told her to wait for him in the room.

She sat on the bed and waited. And waited and waited. Airplanes roared overhead in a place where nobody knew who she was. She sat and enjoyed the silence between takeoffs. What would they do with the money he'd make? Would there be a big party? She had no grand plans. She was thirteen years old, just along for the ride.

Two hours turned into four, then six. She played with the TV but grew bored, then suspicious. Hours passed and still no call, no knock, no key in the door. After eight hours, she was certain something had gone wrong. Greg wasn't coming back. Rather than sit there and wait to get caught by who knows what—or be stuck with the bill for the room—she pried the fire extinguisher case off the wall, stashed the mescaline in her backpack, and rode the elevator down to the lobby, which was deserted. No sign of Greg. She slipped out the front door and stuck her thumb in the direction of Cambridge.

Megan had in her possession a decent amount of mescaline that seemed to belong to nobody. Did finders-keepers apply to an abandoned stash? Would someone come looking for it? For her? It was best to get rid of it as soon as possible.

She didn't have the money to buy empty capsules, so she portioned the powder out by wrapping doses in little toilet paper packets just big enough to place under your tongue. She twisted the edges closed and sold them out of her backpack in the Common for $4 per generous hit. She paid up the rent for her room under the stairs and spent the rest on a pair of Frye harness boots, butternut leather, the stacked heel making her an even 5'10". With Tommy's black velvet cape, now she had a look.

After the mescaline heist, Cambridge felt compromised. Megan spent a month looking over her shoulder. Would Greg come back for his stash? What would happen to her if he did? Or worse, what if the intended buyers found her? Another girl said she was going to New York. Did Megan want to ride with her? Hell yes.

When she got there, she stepped out of the car and into a city lit up for the Christmas season as if it had been waiting for her this whole time. She walked up to the first group of freaks she saw and asked what she always did: "Where do you like to hang out?"

It wasn't the grandeur of the midtown skyscrapers or the neon of Broadway beckoning. As soon as Megan stepped onto St. Mark's Place, she knew she was home. Boston and Cambridge seemed drab and provincial by comparison—too many scarves and textbooks and long memories. New York lacked the altitudinal beauty of Aspen, of course—trashcans overflowed, the November smell of kitchen garbage and pee was now a tenacious haint, and broken glass dusted the sidewalks like aborted sugar work—but the wildness of it all stirred something in Megan similar to how she felt back in the Rockies, which seemed like years ago but had only been three months. She wouldn't have named the edge in the air as a reverberation of four people having just been murdered inside Nadja's, the Polish bar on Avenue A—owner Nadja Puczynski, along with a bartender and two unlucky patrons, had found themselves at the center of a hold-up near closing time when one of the robbers opened fire without warning—but she felt the city's paradox on an instinctive level. Here was community and anonymity in harmony, everything she had sought on her journey, plus all the kaleidoscopic sensory delights a kid could want.

Megan's New York was psychedelia at the Electric Circus, which was already on its way out by then, though she never cared about what tastemakers thought. It was the Fillmore East: no ticket, no money, no problem. It was scrounging for change in Tompkins Square Park to a bongo backbeat for an egg cream at Gem Spa or an Acapulco Gold at the Ice Cream Connection. Never mind that its intoxicating properties came solely from the freshness of the peaches shot through with "hash" flakes of chocolate. The sign on the wall read, "The World

So Made Is Still Being Made and Getting More Beautiful Every Day," and, taking small bites of her peach and chocolate-flake ice cream to make it last as long as possible, Megan would have told anyone that she wholeheartedly agreed. Her version of New York was heading next door to the East Side Bookstore to thumb through underground comics, R. Crumb's denizens and the Fabulous Furry Freak Brothers of *Feds 'n' Heads* emerging out of an alternate inked universe from the Superman and Archie books on the spinner racks of the stores she'd known before, the *Zap #4* obscenity trial possibly making the clerks nervous when the door would open, not knowing who would walk in and see a kid like her near the merchandise.

Megan's New York was sleeping where she could, when she could—on the steps to the subway on bad nights, in the Earth People's commune in an abandoned building on Fourth or Fifth Street on good ones. "Hey, Earth People! Hey, Earth People! Send me a key!" she would call up from the sidewalk, and sure enough, it would work. A woman would lean out a window and lower a key down on a string that got her into the building where there must have been eighty people humming inside like happy bees, ready to ladle her up a bowl of brown rice and beans, point her to a corner of a room, and let her grab a safe night's sleep. As she tucked her backpack under her head and relaxed, finally, into the hive's gentle buzz, she would feel a peace she hadn't felt since those summer nights in Aspen's Wagner Park, like she'd unlocked all the secrets that her parents, her teachers, and the entire hat-and-tie-wearing world had been keeping from her.

She had licked the city in record time, figured out how to hop the turnstile and ride uptown for free to watch the ice skaters in Central Park, then walk through the marbled lobbies of the grand hotels on Fifth Avenue and act like she belonged there, noticing how different she looked from the dressed-up girls barely older than her who would float between the dining rooms and lounges. She'd stand up a little taller, throw her shoulders back, and look everyone directly in the eye. Visibility was a kind of invisibility, she learned. If it was Saturday, that was good for long-distance calls, so she would tuck herself into a lobby phone booth, pull a slip of paper out of her bag with the formula for a DIY telephone credit card spread through underground papers and guerilla theater skits (any phone number, plus 158, worked if you wanted to rip off Ma Bell), and she'd dial the number for the house in Atchison.

"Mmhello?" Her mother's voice, soft as a cashmere coat, always sounded far away on the line.

She never knew what to say, ever, so she always hung up right away.

Calling home made her aware of how alone she was in the city. In Cambridge, the kids stuck together on the street, but New York was wholly unconcerned with her. She was just another new kid with a backpack. She wished she had someone to talk to. She remembered this cute boy she had met back home the previous summer; we'll call him Steven. She figured he must live nearby. He was out of school and traveling around the country when they met. He had told her he was from New York. He had taken her around the county fairgrounds and shown her how the games were rigged—a fun and sweet and flirty day, all very innocent and thrilling. They exchanged addresses and even wrote each other a few letters after he had returned home. Struck by the realization that she was now close enough to visit, she picked up the phone and dialed information.

Steven sounded surprised but happy to hear from her—the opposite of how she imagined her mother would have reacted had Megan said hello back. He called her by her real name.

"You should take the train out to Long Island," he said, offering to meet her at the Oceanside station. "We can find a party. And I'll show you the ocean."

She boarded the LIRR at Penn Station, and when the train emerged from underground, she was surprised to see that the city had faded away, replaced by regular houses and stores, towns that looked like places to be from, not places to go toward. Steven was waiting for her in the train station parking lot, leaning on an old pickup truck.

"You made it," he said, helping her into the truck's cab. "I didn't know if you'd really come."

"I said I would, silly," she said with a laugh, slinging her backpack onto the floorboard and turning her bright smile his way. "Didn't I?"

It felt good to talk to someone she recognized, even someone she knew mostly from chatty letters, whom she'd only spent one afternoon with a year ago, a lifetime ago.

"You're going to have to tell me everything you've done since you left Kansas. I bet it's been wild," he said. "But first—I have something for you."

He reached his closed fist out to her. She placed her hand under his and he dropped a few bright red capsules, one at a time, into her open palm.

"What are these?" she asked.

They looked like Hot Tamales, the cinnamon candies you could buy at the movies that burned your tongue and turned it bright red if you ate too many at once.

"You've never had reds?" he asked. "They just help you relax."

The relaxing was half the fun of anything; a little hash or wine always made it easier to forget that she was supposed to care that she didn't know where she might sleep on any given night, or that it had been a while since she'd heard that "mmhello?" on the other end of the line. She had gotten into the habit of accepting what was offered, and it had served her well. What the hell? She threw the capsules into her mouth and swallowed.

She woke up to pain and a man's face above her that she didn't recognize. Her eyes were open, but she was trapped. She couldn't move. She looked left and right and saw boxes; it was a storage room of some kind. She didn't know where she was, where Steven was, who the face above her belonged to, or how long she had been like that. She faded back out. When she woke again, Steven was there, along with some other man. Who? Her arms were slung over their shoulders, and they were walking her between them, dragging her really, through a door. Then the blackness overtook her again. The next time she became aware of the room around her, she saw the rust reds and moss greens and wood paneling of a motel room before drifting back under. It was a struggle to keep her head above the black water, and every time she surfaced, she saw and felt nothing but pain and horror.

There were four of them, and they kept her steadily slipping out of consciousness almost as soon as she would wake up. They pulled shifts with her. They never left her alone.

Just once, their timing was off. One man had fallen asleep on the motel bed with nobody else in the room. As he snored next to her, she wiggled her toes and fingers and found she could move. She turned over and inched toward the edge of the bed, swinging her legs around until her feet touched shag carpet. If she didn't get out of there now, she might not ever. The man stirred slightly, heaved a large snore, and she froze until his breathing became rhythmic again. Her eyes adjusted to the low light. She stood up and tiptoed around the room, pulling on her dress and grabbing her boots and backpack off the floor where they had been dropped. She turned the doorknob a hair's width at a time, praying that the sleeping man would not hear her and that another man would not be waiting on the other side.

She slipped out the door and onto the balcony of the motel and back into the banality of the outside world. She didn't look back as she ran, barefoot, down the metal stairs and across the parking lot.

The first thing she saw at the mouth of the lot was a police cruiser parked at the curb. *I have to tell somebody*, she thought. *I have to tell him what they did to me.* Then she imagined jail again; the phone call to her mother, the "mmhello?" on the other end turning from relief to anger to disbelief. Then she thought about her mother being told something she couldn't unknow, something she would see every time Megan walked into the room, something her father would have to be told too.

She picked up her pace even as the rough pavement stung, but she forgot she had boots in her hand that would stop the pain on the soles of her feet. If the cop, or anyone else for that matter, saw a barefoot girl running down a sidewalk that evening like the devil had just fallen asleep on the job, they didn't say or do anything to stop her.

When she got far enough away, and around enough people that she felt safe slowing down, she did what she knew how to do: she stuck out her thumb, looking for a ride back into the city. She waved three men past before a woman, older than her but younger than her mother, stopped. Megan got in. She locked the door and pulled the sun visor down and studied her face in the vanity mirror. No bruises she could see. Her body was sore, but her arms and legs worked; she could run. She thought, in a really fucked up way, that maybe she had been lucky. She had been unconscious for most of it, so they hadn't hurt her as badly as they could have.

The woman lit a cigarette and offered her one.

"What day is it?" Megan asked her.

"It's Tuesday," the woman said, giving her a long look as she pulled away from the curb. "Are you okay?"

Megan's brain still felt foggy, and she knew she looked and sounded fucked up. But if she acted like it was no big deal and kept her cool, maybe she could get on with her life. Here is what she decided that day, and she has kept this mantra ever since: This wasn't going to change her. It didn't have to if she didn't let it.

She wasn't going to explain herself to anyone, ever.

Besides, nobody ever wants to hear a true answer to that question.

"Yeah, it's no big deal," Megan said, taking the cigarette. "I just need to get back to the city."

There are events that stick with you even though you have no reason to believe you need to file them away in your memory catalog. I was sixteen, and my mother and I had just had a fight. Correction: I did not fight with her; rather, she had just finished yelling at me for some overblown event while I cried. Throughout my childhood, she was often angry, disproportionately so to the nature of my childish, obnoxiously casual, teenage offenses. That afternoon, a friend of mine rang the doorbell. She had two boys from another school waiting out in her car, and she wanted to know if I could take a ride out to the lake with her, with them. I didn't know the boys—they weren't just from another school, they seemed a little rough, from outside of our usual artsy-nerdy circle, and I wasn't interested—and neither did my mother. My face was a mess, and I wasn't in the mood, but more than that, I was sure my mother wouldn't let me go. A grounding after a blow-up was more her style. But Mom's mood changed almost immediately. She gave her permission easily, cheerfully even, as soon as my friend promised only she would drive, and when I said I didn't really feel like being social, she still made me go upstairs and change and practically shoved me out the door. At the time, I thought she was trying to say she was sorry for losing her temper, and it annoyed me even more that she didn't seem to realize that kicking me out to hang out with some random guys I had no interest in would not do the job. Decades later, when she finally told me the story of the motel, I understood that she sent me out as insurance, as an extra pair of eyes and ears, a loud girl with no patience for bullshit boys. I was there to keep my friend safe.

While I was in college, my mother, who worked as a labor and delivery nurse until she had to retire due to a back injury, became a certified sexual assault nurse examiner, the first at her hospital, on call to perform rape kits. She held the hands of women and girls while she collected the evidence of what had happened to them. She listened; she took notes. She witnessed their pain. She testified in court when they pressed charges. She gave them the assurance of a record: something terrible had been done to them, and now someone knew.

I don't know who the other three men in the motel were. I have Steven's real name. I once found a phone number I thought might lead me to him. But I don't think it's my place to investigate further.

———————————

Megan needed a coat. It was December, for Christ's sake, and there was no pretending she could get by with just her jean jacket. But the first thing she bought with the first few dollars she panhandled wasn't the afghan coat she had her eye on in a St. Mark's boutique. She bought a knife, small enough to stay hidden but long enough to do damage if need be. This capitulation to the world hurt; her vow of nonviolence that had felt so important just three months earlier— important enough to sacrifice her own skin, her entire life—now felt like a relic from a childhood she couldn't quite remember. But better to hurt than be hurt like that again.

With the knife in her pocket, she felt bold enough to put her smile back on, open her eyes wide, and try to get to twenty dollars for that afghan coat, one quarter at a time.

"Hey, man, sorry to bother you, but could you spare a quarter?" she asked as a couple brushed by her without stopping.

"Megan? Megan! Megan from Boston!"

She spun around and saw him: Gabe, who used to hang out at the house in Cambridge. Gabe, with the head of curls and the sweetheart smile who could do Joe Cocker at Woodstock better than even Joe Cocker could.

"What are you doing here?" she asked.

"Winter break," he said. "What are you doing right now?"

"Making some money," she said, shaking the cup in her hand at him. "I want to buy a coat."

"That's not enough," he said, eyeballing her change. "It's going to take forever. Let me try."

Rich boys are natural beggars. People love to give what they can sense you don't need.

As they panhandled together, easily reaching Megan's goal, Gabe mentioned in passing that he wasn't planning on going back to Boston. He didn't say why, and she didn't ask. They didn't really talk about anything that had happened before whatever day it happened to be, which is one reason why he felt like a safe harbor. He walked everywhere easily, like he belonged. They ran around the city together, both lives suspended mercifully in the winter's crystal air. He slipped a small brass pig into her pocket one afternoon, and when they weren't together, she would reach in and hold it in her palm, the compact weight of it reassuring her that she had at least one friend in the world, and he was real.

Gabe had a home in the city, a past and a family to anchor him, and when Megan walked into his building on the Upper West Side, she could tell they had money. They kissed and held hands on his mother's gold sectional sofa, the plastic slipcover squeaking under her thighs. After the terror of the motel, she welcomed Gabe's sweetness. They curled up in his childhood bed together and she allowed herself to sleep.

One afternoon, they were listening to records in his room and heard the front door unlock. The door to Gabe's bedroom flew open, and his mother raged when she saw Megan sitting on the bed.

"You," she said. Her tone was accusatory and personal, even though Megan had never met her. "Megan from Cambridge, the infamous Megan!"

Gabe's father started shouting at him about his future. His mother's voice continued to rise.

"You're the reason why he's not going back to college," she said. "This is your fault. He dropped out because of you!"

"She didn't have anything to do with it," Gabe protested, but his mother wasn't hearing it. She picked up one of Gabe's cowboy boots and hit him on the shoulder with it. "This is her fault!"

Megan had no idea why Gabe had dropped out or if he even had. Whatever had gone down in Boston hadn't involved her. Gabe's mother kept smacking him with the business end of the boot. He grabbed Megan's hand and pulled her past his parents into the hallway. His mother followed, swinging the boot at Megan this time, catching her on the arm with the heel.

"This is your fault!" she screamed.

Now she was chasing them, swinging the boot, and if it hadn't been utterly terrifying to Megan, not to mention supremely unfair, it might have been funny. Gabe pulled Megan along by the hand, and they ran out the apartment's front door together, his mother screaming at him to come back and fix this now.

A neighbor popped his head out into the hallway, took one look at Gabe's mother tearing down the hall, and pulled the kids inside, locking his door behind them.

"Children," this middle-aged man in a sweater said calmly. "What on Earth?"

He poured them each a Scotch and let them sit down and catch their breath. Megan and Gabe took their drinks and sipped gratefully. Megan's hands were shaking.

"It's really not your fault," Gabe told her.

"I know that," she laughed, bewildered by the entire scene. Of all the things that she felt were her fault, this one was on him.

She set her drink down and walked over to the man's stereo. To call it a stereo would be to call the Plaza "a hotel"—she'd never seen anything like it before: floor-to-ceiling gear, giant speakers, a stereosonic open-reel tape player in addition to a turntable. It took her breath away. She ran her finger across the spines of a shelf of albums. He had everything, everyone, right here in his living room.

"Who do you like?" the neighbor asked.

"Jefferson Airplane. Jimi Hendrix. Carole King," she said.

The neighbor scanned his shelves, pulling out album after album and stacking them on the table.

"I'll fix you up," he said.

As a little girl, Megan had once walked across the old market square in Rouen where Joan of Arc had been burned. The sudden rush of understanding that there could be too much music for one person's life reminded her of that feeling, of how small she was within the world's wonder and terror. While Gabe poked his head out the door to see if the coast was clear, she gathered up the albums and thanked the neighbor. It was almost Christmas, and she might not have a record player, or a place to have a record player even, but at least she had the start of a good collection. For every disaster, a little miracle in return, as if the city always knew the minimum of what she needed to keep going.

———

"Mmhello?"

It was Christmas Day, and Megan was sitting inside one of her wooden hotel lobby phone booths, twisting the cord in her fingers. She decided not to hang up this time.

"Mommy, it's me."

"Where are you?" her mother demanded. "When are you coming home?"

"I don't know, Mommy," she said. "Merry Christmas."

"Well, you'd better come home now," she said. "We're moving."

Megan was used to moving every twelve to eighteen months—that was the one constant in an Army family, and it had been true for them her entire life—but the news still caught her off guard. She had lost track of how long she had been gone and how long her father had been deployed.

"Did you hear me?" her mother asked. "The movers have been here. The house is packed up and we are ready to go. Your father's coming home. We're leaving soon to pick him up in California. Now where in the hell are you?"

Megan told her.

"And how are you going to get home?" her mother asked.

It's not that she expected her mother to drop everything—the movers, her brothers, turning the rental house back over to the landlords, preparing herself for the return of a husband who had once again been at war—but hitchhiking alone in late December, standing on the side of the highway in the bitter cold, vulnerable, with the nights coming so quickly, after the motel—it was overwhelming to think about. She had never thought of Kansas as permanent, because of course no place was for her family, but she wasn't ready to feel them scattered to the winds without her. And her father was coming home. He had made it through his tour, and so had she.

"I don't know, Mommy," she said. "But I'll find a way."

Later, she snuck over to Gabe's and beamed when he set a gift-wrapped box down on the kitchen table—a Christmas present from her boyfriend was a delightful surprise. She ran her hands over the folded tissue paper, then pulled a floor-length, empire-waisted black velvet dress out of the box, holding it up to her shoulders and twirling the skirt around.

"It's the most beautiful dress I've ever seen," she told him. His kindness crushed her, and it lifted her up.

At the end of the evening, she told him.

"I need to go home. My parents are moving."

The next day, he told her it was all taken care of. His parents were more than happy to buy her a plane ticket to Kansas City. They would even take her to the airport.

She wore the black Christmas dress with her Frye boots and the panhandled Afghan coat. She carried the records his neighbor had given her, and her backpack was loaded with everything else that was hers. Gabe walked her to the gate, and his parents came with them, probably to see her get on the plane and out of their son's life with their own eyes. From her window seat, she saw Gabe standing in the window overlooking the tarmac, and she raised one hand to the glass. He lifted his arms up and held them out like wings, as if he was the plane lifting her up, up into the air, and kept them there until she did. Then Megan Shane vanished for the final time.

5
Taking Off

Megan disappeared into the sky over New York, and my mother landed in Kansas to rejoin her family, only to leave immediately for California to pick up her father. The Colonel was home from Vietnam, and the family would be moving to North Carolina and a new Army base. I imagine my mother moving through the new house filled with the unpacked gilded furniture, heavy oil still life paintings, and ornate antique weaponry my grandparents collected, stopping to trail her finger along the Airborne mascot. That's the one thing of the Colonel's I wanted after he died; not the butter-colored two-seater Triumph TR6 he only took out of the garage on beautiful days, and not the creamy baby grand piano that once graced the saloon of a Kansas City whorehouse, which I never in my life saw anyone play. I wanted what sat on top of the piano: a human skull wearing the maroon beret of a US Army Airborne Division, proudly displayed along with framed family photographs. A skull wearing a beret is a classic Death from Above motif, and my grandfather's company had its own variation: theirs had dice for eyes, a tribute to both luck and when it runs out. I didn't even want to ask for the beret, figuring it would be precious to my mother or her brother. I just wanted the skull. I didn't know at the time that the anonymous dead person's head I had grown up admiring, stolen from a village graveyard somewhere near St-André-de-l'Eure in the early 1960s, would be gone by the time I thought to ask for it.

The Colonel told the story often: how he decided he needed an actual human skull to grace his desk back when he had been promoted to captain. (Even knowing this, I can't think of him as any rank other than colonel; it's what we called him and how we thought of him, by his highest rank.) He enlisted his friend Jack to help, and together, they walked to the village cemetery, scaled the wall, broke into the charnel house, and selected one by hand. So maybe they had been drinking. The Colonel went back over the wall first and called to his friend from the street below.

"Throw him here, Jack!"

And Jack, looking up over the top of the wall, pulled his arm back and threw the human head like a football. It soared over the Colonel's head and smashed into a hundred pieces in the street. They had to act fast, before someone came to check on the commotion.

"Well, go get another one!" the Colonel yelled back.

The next skull Jack pulled from the pile of bones dropped down smooth and easy into the Colonel's waiting hands. Then they ran.

The skull traveled with him from desk to desk across France, then to the family's next post in Germany, and after that from home to home, base to base. At some point, they acquired the piano and completed the tableau, a visual aid for a story to tell whenever he had an audience. It wouldn't have occurred to me to question the morality of graverobbing in the name of style. Questioning the Colonel wasn't done.

He styled himself after John Wayne: cowboy swagger meets soldier discipline with a thousand-yard judgmental stare. He loved war movies and Westerns, and we watched them all with him from an early age. In both genres, Wayne embodied a taciturn masculinity of which the Colonel approved. I became partial to one of his favorite Westerns, John Ford's *The Man Who Shot Liberty Valance*, which taught me that a convenient story can become more powerful than the truth if it's given enough credence. In this film, John Wayne plays Tom Doniphon, the rancher who rescues Jimmy Stewart's Ranse Stoddard after he's beaten by the violent gang terrorizing their little town of Shinbone. Stoddard becomes the public face of heroism, and a senator, after he's credited with shooting Liberty Valance and ridding Shinbone of this scourge. He gets the girl, the office, and the legend. Doniphon, meanwhile, the man who really pulled the trigger, gets nothing but the satisfaction of doing the job. His is a silent, noble suffering, the ultimate test of manhood. It is also a cruel fiction, built on complicity and requiring a willing target, a scapegoat to suffer the degradation of the truth.

If a hero narrative can be fabricated to override the truth, so can narratives of victim and villain. There is something about a shocking story that makes us not want to question its logic, as if answers might burst the story's dark magic. Take my mother running away from home while the Colonel was at war. A certain kind of child will decide, if she is made to take care of the hardest problems herself, to refuse any limits on her freedom that feel arbitrary, even frivolous, in light of her responsibilities. It is impossible for me to know this story and not feel on some level that she also ran away in order to be seen, even in her absence. On the road as Megan, my mother put herself into increasingly dangerous scenarios until the unthinkable happened when she took that train to Oceanside. And although I do not believe these events were cosmically related, after getting beaten up at school, after the Boston jail, after the hungry December nights on New York City subway station floors, and after the horrors of that motel room, her father did come home alive and intact, with war stories with which to regale the family, a new home in North Carolina, and a path to promotion to lieutenant colonel.

After she came home at Christmas in 1970, my mother tried to settle back into military family life. But a wildness had taken root in her, and that spring, mere months after returning, she left her family again, this time with a plan to return to New York with another new name and all the street smarts she had lost so much to gain the year before. She stayed gone. Nobody, as far as anyone has ever admitted in our family, went looking for her, a mere eight hours up I-95. Over time, my mother the runaway became the antagonist in my family's story during that period: the willful child who permanently disrupted the peace. My mother would later spend the rest of her parents' lives making it up to them. And I have spent years trying to understand why, when she was the child and the Colonel was the commanding officer, he didn't work harder at keeping her safe once he came home from the war.

Here is a story the Colonel didn't tell us, but which my mother did when I asked her what happened to the skull I wanted so badly that vanished the morning of his funeral. One day in the early 1960s, when the family was posted in Idar-Oberstein, Germany, the Colonel was away from his office, and—as he told it—some pissed-off soldier picked that tangible symbol of his command off the desk and threw it to the ground, where it smashed into a hundred pieces, just like its predecessor that had been left in the street outside the village cemetery.

The Colonel was, of course, irate. The disrespect. Nobody in the company would admit to the desecration of the already-desecrated item. He ordered the remains swept up but reserved, then went to the quartermaster and placed a special request for the woodshop. And when his order was ready, he placed the remains of the skull inside a tiny handmade coffin and commanded the entire company assemble for a burial. The bugler played "Taps" as the company finally committed the skull, purloined in Normandy, to the ground in Germany. But that doesn't explain how the Death from Above skull came to be on the baby grand during my childhood, decades later. How, when I asked my mother for it after she had nursed the Colonel from diagnosis to death of lung cancer in 2007—an echo of how, nine years earlier, she had taken care of Grandmother between the stroke that incapacitated her and the one that finally killed her so the Colonel wouldn't have to treat the love of his life like an invalid but could just be her husband in their final days together, a double act of love and sacrifice—she told me that she wished she had known I had wanted it before his funeral.

It had been suggested to my mother that she throw it out while cleaning for the repast. But how? Out the car window on a country drive, perhaps, or just out with the trash? Those options seemed less like solutions to the problem of what to do with this macabre relic and more like a true crime headline waiting to happen: *Human Remains Found in Pasture; DNA Tests Inconclusive.* Instead, she brought the skull to the funeral home in a plastic grocery bag and asked the funeral director, a friend, to place it in her father's left hand before sealing up his casket, and to please not ask any questions. And that's why, if you dig up and crack open the Colonel's casket now, you will find the remains of one man with two heads. Like some mythical being, two men's egos attached to one headstone.

The Colonel may have admired Tom Doniphon, the unsung hero of *The Man Who Shot Liberty Valance*, but he did not emulate him. The Colonel, as the skull story shows, was a man who took credit. He told his own story; he held court. He loved stories about individuals who stamped out lawlessness with violence, who stood perpetually on the edge of civilized society, sure they would lose something elemental by joining it and yet remaining jealously protective of it, their identities forged as saviors of that which they were so ambivalent toward. He, on the other hand, was very much a believer in America and the military-industrial complex that allowed him to work his way up to a life of privilege. For the Army, he was the ultimate company man: he enlisted in 1953, graduated from officer candidate school as a second lieutenant in 1961, and was assigned to the 101st Airborne Division as platoon leader. His work took the family all over France and Germany before he went to Vietnam the first time, in 1966, to serve as an interrogation officer. He ended his active duty at the Pentagon, working for the Office of the Inspector General as a fraud, waste, and abuse inspector. Later, he came out of retirement to work as a military analyst for a defense contractor. A certain kind of man— the kind, perhaps, who has spent time as both a wartime interrogator and a fraud, waste, and abuse inspector—likes to see himself as the last, fierce bulwark between chaos and order in the world. Or, in his more irritable moments, the only one with any goddamned sense. A hero, whether you asked for one or not.

A hero is not always a good man, because he doesn't have to be. In Ford's 1956 film *The Searchers*, John Wayne plays Ethan, a former Confederate soldier living on the margins as a suspected outlaw, an "angrier, and more troubled than ever" John Wayne character, writes Glenn Frankel, author of *The Searchers: The Making of an American Legend*: "This dark knight is determined to exterminate the damsel and anyone who stands in his way." The plot of *The Searchers* may revolve around his kidnapped niece Debbie (Natalie Wood) and the years-long quest to recover her from the Comanche who took her captive after killing the rest of her family of Texican settlers in a raid. But the story is not about her; it's about Ethan's drive to eliminate the Comanche and reclaim what has been stolen—in this case, a girl who may or may not be his daughter.

The Searchers was inspired by the story of a real girl, Cynthia Ann Parker, a nine-year-old girl who was kidnapped from her white family of East Texas settlers during a Comanche raid in 1836. Raised among the Comanche, she eventually became the wife of a warrior and the mother of three children. Among Texans, she became an obsession, then a legend. Her story, Frankel writes, "had been told and retold, altered and reimagined, by each generation to fit its own needs and sensibility, until fact and fiction had blended together to form a foundational American myth."

A 1954 novelization of the Cynthia Ann Parker story by Alan Le May turned the focus away from the girl and toward the men of her family who pledged to reclaim her. This is a novelist's prerogative, to flip the perspective of a well-known story toward an underexplored point of view. Rather than write another version of the captivity narrative, Le May centered his novel, also called *The Searchers*, on Parker's uncle's quest for rescue and vengeance. And in so doing, the story of Cynthia Ann became a vehicle for a complicated man's redemption and sacrificial exile.

Although the story of Cynthia Ann has long been a robust part of Texas history, as Jan Reid wrote in *Texas Monthly* in 2003, the legend and the fact are miles apart: "Even as Cynthia Ann is celebrated—in histories, novels, movies, children's literature, and opera—she continues to be mythologized." Cynthia Ann's reality, Reid writes, little resembled the story men crafted out of her survival: "It is said that she was beautiful (in fact the years of hard living had been punishing), that she was a tragic victim (in fact she cherished her life with the Comanches), that she was a slave to an evil warrior (in fact she loved her husband deeply). Indeed, much of what has been said about her is fiction." At least once, Cynthia Ann—also named Naduah, or Narua—escaped white society to return to the Comanche community she loved.

What the Le May's novel and Ford's adaptation did—elevating the motivations and struggles of the men, while relegating Debbie to a flattened version of a mythical Cynthia Ann—matters beyond the film's closing credits. As critic Stuart Byron observes "all recent American cinema derives from John Ford's *The Searchers*." In 2008, the American Film Institute named it the greatest American western. These days, outside Texas, the story of Cynthia Ann Parker is a footnote in the history of a fictionalized film about the imagined inner lives of the men who pursued her, a foundational text influencing the most significant popular filmmakers of the twentieth century, who continue to shape prevalent notions of gender, freedom, justice, and redemption. The film's influence looms large in the works of Steven Spielberg, George Lucas, and Martin Scorsese—the men who told the stories about morality and honor I grew up consuming. In an interview from the AFI Archive, Scorsese remembers seeing *The Searchers* for the first time as a kid. "[Ethan's] terrifying," he recalls. "He literally acts out the worst aspects of racism in our country, and it's right there. You could see the hate. You could see it building. You could also see how he could go that way . . . he becomes obsessive."

You could also see how he could go that way because of whose perspective Ford's film privileges. (Scorsese does grapple at length with the film's complexities and cruelties, especially its treatment of a Comanche woman Debbie's adopted brother Martin mistakenly weds, in a 2013 guest review for the *Hollywood Reporter*.) Debbie's life with the Comanche is left to the audience's most lurid, violent imaginations. To Ethan, rescuing Debbie means killing her. Because she has been living as one of the wives to the Comanche chief, Scar, Ethan would be putting an end to a life he does not see as worth living. Perhaps she knows this on some level because when Ethan and Martin find her the first time, she turns them away. With as few options as she has in that moment, Debbie decides she is not going to be anyone's sacrifice. A switch is flipped, and Debbie goes from missing girl to runaway, from a tragedy to a problem to be solved.

The film indicts Ethan's racism, but mostly through the lens of how it affects him, how his unresolved hate and refusal to consider himself part of the Union, literally and figuratively, corrodes his spirit, hardens his heart, and basically dooms him to the wandering life of a lonely bachelor.

"Is the film intended to endorse their attitudes, or to dramatize and regret them?" Roger Ebert asked in his review of the film. "Today we see it through enlightened eyes, but in 1956, many audiences accepted its harsh view of Indians. Ford knew that his hero's hatred of Indians was wrong, but his glorification of Ethan's search invites admiration for a twisted man."

Add that glorification to the John Wayne mystique, and little wonder if the film didn't land with its full potential weight upon its audience at the time. The Colonel watched *The Searchers* as a conservative white man of that era watching a John Wayne Western, which is to say, not through what Ebert called "enlightened eyes." And through that lens, one trained on the film's protagonist, *The Searchers* poses another question for a man to ponder: Do you allow a missing girl to become an obsession, to ruin your life, or do you move on and focus your energy on conserving the remaining resources at the settlement?

In the end, Ethan has killed Scar and grabbed Debbie, and they are riding away from the Comanche camp when he has a change of heart. The old racist soldier ends up showing this girl, his own kin, mercy. That's how we know he's the protagonist of the story: the changes he experiences are the ones that count.

In the final scene, Debbie, her face stricken with fear, is carried into the next chapter of her life, her uncertain recovery. We don't get to see her reentry into Texican life, nor do we see her work through the trauma her experiences have left her with. The men have found her and brought her home, and she is now "safe," end of story. The closing shot instead lingers on Ethan, hat askew, framed by the cabin's doorway, bathed in light, unwilling to follow her inside and into the next stage where she must, for the second time in her short life, reorient her entire world. The door closes on Ethan, the one who searches—for what he believes is justice, for a place in the world that will honor a man like him, and we know there are many such places— as he walks away into the wide-open country.

Why am I talking about the Colonel and the movies he loved instead of my mother? I keep circling back to the stories that should have been told about girls and women but instead were given over to men, and my own complicity in perpetuating these narrative imbalances and injustices. In a workshop in graduate school, a classmate said of my writing, during a discussion portion of the class when I was not allowed to speak, "These poems are very concerned with the male perspective." Her tone intimated that was a bad thing. I wrote poems to try to understand the world and my place in it. The male perspective set the agenda, as far as I could see, from public desire to injustices perpetrated in its name. I didn't know what, or even how, to want apart from its influence. I couldn't say that. How could I admit such a thing out loud, in an academic setting, in the early twenty-first century? I knew enough to keep my mouth shut. At the end, when I was given a chance to respond, I took my cues from the more experienced writers around me and simply said, "Thank you." I tried to mean it.

When I return to the question of why my mother was allowed to stay gone for so long, I return to the idea of resources. My grandparents were many things, but above all, they were conservative capitalist white Americans, true believers in the system that allowed them to earn beyond their humble beginnings and assemble the affluent lives they desired. How their children presented themselves mattered; it reflected the family's fitness for upward mobility. When my mother moved with her family to North Carolina after her time as Megan, it could have been easier for her there than it had been in Kansas— they were back where a father's rank counted, back where all the kids were new kids at some point. But gossip about her ensured it wasn't. When a missing girl is found, she's transformed into a miracle. A runaway remains a fugitive even after she's home. The other kids were forbidden to talk to her, as if her status might have been contagious. What she had done reflected poorly on her father. That was the primary concern, and so her movements were tightly controlled. She was a reminder of how precarious their life was, how quickly it could all fall apart for her parents, her brother, their futures.

The second time she left, she went back to New York and didn't come back. Her little brother told his classmates in North Carolina that she was away at boarding school. Years later, as she flipped through a photo album from that era, a clipping from the army base newspaper fell out: a photo of the front yard of her parents' house in Fort Bragg. They had won an award for the most beautiful garden. The write-up noted that the Colonel and his wife had two sons. She had been written out of their story.

———————

Had I grown up with access to art house movies instead of cable TV and bootleg VHS tapes, I might have encountered a different narrative of parents looking for missing kids. Before Miloš Forman made his Academy Award-winning adaptation of *One Flew Over the Cuckoo's Nest*, he made the dark comedy *Taking Off*. Released in 1971, the Czech director's first American film won the Grand Prix at Cannes and was the subject of several *New York Times* stories, but in a year when *Fiddler on the Roof*, *The Last Picture Show*, *The French Connection*, *Dirty Harry*, and *A Clockwork Orange* were among the top box office hits, Forman's comedy failed to make a mark in wide release. To this day, copies are difficult to find in the States. As I write this, it's still not streaming on any platform, and the DVD versions are all coded for European players, making it difficult for Forman fans to see this bridge between his European New Wave origins and his Oscar-winning Hollywood career. I ordered my bootleg copy from an online store whose form and function seemed to be frozen in the early dot-com days, a digital version of the indie video stores whose stock was curated by cinephile clerks before Blockbuster, then Netflix, put most of them out of business.

Taking Off is a mirror-flipped picaresque, a satire of suburban middle-class parenting in which the adults are the ones smoking, flirting, and drinking their way through what should be a sobering search for their missing teenagers. When people talk about *Taking Off*, they often focus on the opening scene, which is incredibly hilarious and disturbing and perhaps not memed into oblivion only because not enough digital natives have been able to see it to get the reference. In it, a series of earnest teenage girls sing increasingly unhinged songs for what we later learn is an audition. Anyone who has seen this montage will mention a young Carly Simon performing and Kathy Bates (billed as Bobo Bates) singing a deranged parody of a folk song about winged horses. (The soundtrack is absolute lunacy, hard to find except on vinyl. My husband groaned when my secondhand copy arrived in the mail.) It is to this audition that fifteen-year-old Jeannie (a luminous Linnea Heacock) has gone without permission, and from which she doesn't return, sending her parents, Larry and Lynn (Buck Henry and Lynn Carlin, who are brilliant) into a tailspin. Larry and his friend head out to look for Jeannie while the wives stay home in case she calls, but in stark contrast to *The Searchers*, the hapless guys just end up at the bar. Jeannie makes it home that night, but it's a whole scene.

Lynn inspects her arm, demanding to know what drugs she's on. Jeannie and Larry face off, and Larry hits her, demanding of Lynn, "Does she know what a great father she has?" Jeannie hardly has any lines, but Heacock's face says everything. Here is a painfully young girl on the first of many potentially dangerous outings, and her parents are bumbling fools.

Jeannie soon slips away again. Larry and Lynn fall in with the Society for the Parents of Fugitive Children, where they learn how to smoke pot from Vincent Schiavelli. They watch Ike and Tina perform a brilliant rendition of "Goodbye, So Long" and have various campy near misses of the sexual variety, including a game of strip poker with fellow SFPFC members that culminates with Larry, stark naked, standing on top of their card table, singing an aria from *La Traviata* when Jeannie comes home again. *Taking Off* dares to say the quiet part about runaways out loud—"Fugitive Children"—and as Steve Lippman writes for *Talk House*, "The film's bold assertion is that [the parents are] liberated, and perhaps happier, without their daughter." The world Jeannie has slipped into is portrayed as dangerous, and it is, but the world of the adults is painted as absurd, grotesque, indulgent, drunken, horny, and ironically childish.

"Were you with a boy?" Larry asks her after he's put on his clothes. He insists Jeannie invite her boyfriend over to dinner. "If he's not a coward, he'll come."

Flash forward. The doorbell rings. Everyone's dressed up, including Jeannie, who wears a lime green minidress, looking every inch the child she still is. In walks not a boy but a grown man with a beard, a musician who, it turns out, makes considerably more per year than Larry does.

"I live very frugally," he tells Jeannie's dismayed parents, with the best line of a film full of brilliant one-liners. "I'm saving up to buy an intercontinental ballistic missile to change the balance of power."

Jeannie continues to say next to nothing, her eyes round as tape reels. Lynn and Larry just shrug, then Larry sings a little Tony Bennett because what else can you do?

I sought out *Taking Off,* hoping to see a dramatized contemporaneous version of my family's experience that wasn't a melodramatic cautionary tale or crime scene. The film's sympathies are neutral, but it spends most of its time with the well-meaning and incompetent Larry and Lynn. Jeannie reacts with silence to her many provocations because Heacock had told Forman that's how she would have responded, and he was looking for a natural performance from her. But for the most part, just like Debbie in *The Searchers,* Jeannie is a conspicuous absence throughout the film, even when she's on screen; yet another girl on the periphery of her own story, even if this one is gentler, more forgiving than the other.

Forman lived in and around the downtown New York scene for a year while making his film. He hung out at the same music venues my mother frequented and invited kids back to the house he rented on Leroy Street in the Village, where he conducted what his housemate, Czech director Ivan Passer, described to the *New York Times* as "amateur sociological research." Although Forman only spent time with one actual runaway—a twelve-year-old girl whose suburbanite parents he contacted on her behalf, only to have them decide she should stay in the city, basically leaving their kid to the unofficial guardianship of a filmmaker—he had long conversations with the teenage children of acquaintances, some of whom had been runaways at one point. He told the *Times* that he "discovered a lot of love, and no understanding. Taken individually, each member of the family would be kind, but when they all got together, they only seemed interested in hurting each other."

So, whose head is buried in the Colonel's hand? Some men tell stories about the fish they couldn't quite reel in or the buck they narrowly missed. My grandfather missed having a skull. Perhaps no more so than after he retired from the Pentagon and moved to Arizona, where he bought a house with a pool and golfed and told stories of his active-duty days. That first Christmas in Yuma, 1980, he received a package. Inside the box, a wrapped hatbox. He removed the wrapping paper, then the lid. Tucked inside a nest of tissue sat a skull. He lit up, lofting the skull up high with one hand, like a Hamlet who had discovered how to cheat death. Up it went onto the baby grand, and by the time we had moved to Yuma a year later, the box in the mail had faded from the story, along with the bespoke miniature casket containing the swept-up shards of the unknown Frenchman's skull, the fed-up enlisted men's rage, the insubordination, and the suggestion that the Colonel had ever been anything but revered by his Airborne men. Erased also was the return address on the Christmas box—ours—and my mother, who by then was twenty-two years old and the mother of two, in formal schooling for the first time since junior high, studying for her LPN, when her program's lead instructor walked into the room with an anatomical skeleton in pieces and asked if anyone wanted part of it before it got thrown out. The other students stared at my mother like she was crazy when she raised her hand and said, "I'll take the head." The only things left in my grandfather's story were the village graveyard, the football spiral, the beret perched atop the skull's smiling face. Grandmother drew a line at the dice in the eye sockets. Maybe she was right. Maybe that thing *was* ghastly enough on its own.

"What is not so well understood about *Liberty Valance*," writes David Coursen in an essay originally published in *Sight and Sound* in 1978, "is its awareness of how the modern world is not simply a betrayal of what preceded it, but a logical extension of it; the flow of history is organic, the present an extension of the past."

I wanted the Colonel's Airborne skull because I needed a little of that daring shine to rub off on me, to give me a prop for a good secondhand story. I wanted to absorb his tale of reckless bravado in pursuit of a mascot for death. I didn't know the object itself was actually a relic of filial devotion, a tribute from the girl whom he had excised so painstakingly from his award-winning yard. I still wish I had it, not for the thrilling origin story I grew up believing it possessed but rather as a talisman of caution and responsibility, a reminder that I control the legend that gets printed now, whose story gets fed to which fire.

6
The Queen of Alphabet City

My mother never thought she'd live to see twenty-one. She told me this as we walked arm-in-arm to the Louvre, discussing her recent diabetes diagnosis. Complications from the disease had shortened her own mother's life, culminating in strokes Grandmother didn't recover from. We were both aware of what the diagnosis could mean. She made this pronouncement about her own mortality often, even after she had lapped her initial prediction the year I graduated college. I was born when she was nineteen, two years after my brother. In a parallel universe where her prophecy had come true, he and I would be orphans, not just fatherless. My mother's continued existence was a dare of sorts to the universe.

The night before, my mother and I had stumbled up the stairs of the Metro station, still groggy from jet lag and the wine we'd had with dinner, on a mission to see just one major site on our first night in Paris. We weren't prepared to see the Eiffel Tower sparkling like it was, a disco dance floor beacon, its famous lightbulbs flashing like midcentury paparazzi. We clutched each other by the arm and nearly collapsed on the sidewalk in giggles: an unexpected moment of magic, over almost as soon as it began, that felt like it had been cued up just for us, a dazzling finger pointing straight up to the sky.

I was almost thirty the year the two of us took that trip to Paris for her forty-ninth birthday, our only vacation with just the two of us. It was my first time; of course, she had been as a child, when her father was stationed in France. We rented an apartment in the Marais and got a little lost in its twisty corridors, stopping to photograph the most beautiful and mysterious of the medieval arrondissement's heavy, gated doors. Crossing the Île de la Cité to take the Metro, we paused in front of Notre Dame, the site of her earliest humiliation. She had been five years old, clutching her mother's hand, when the elastic waistband in her underpants had given out and tumbled down from under her skirt to pool around her ankle socks. A handful of old men clustered around a bench laughed. Tonight, there was no such scene, only me buying our train tickets and consulting my map to get us going in the right direction while she held my elbow to keep me walking at a pace that felt torturous. As a kid, I had learned to walk fast to keep up with her, but now she was slow, deliberate in her steps. She was unsure on the Metro, following my lead in and out of stations, but she stopped to give change to almost every panhandler we passed while I, absorbed in my vacation plans, rolled my eyes at her dawdling, gritting my teeth when I was forced to walk at the pace she preferred.

We of course went to Père Lachaise and paid our respects to Jim Morrison, his headstone littered with bottles and cigarette butts, courtesy of the apostles of rock indulgence. A police officer who was posted to deter such shenanigans beelined for my mother, who still favored capes, a leather backpack, and boots, trappings of a Boomer hippie who might have done god knows what to the rock star's grave. We wandered the narrow lanes and noticed a man in an overcoat, collar flipped up, a scarf tight around his neck, placing scrolls of paper on top of the graves of the famous dead: Apollinaire, Chopin, Proust, Seurat, Colette, Balzac. A couple of kids trailed him, picking them up behind his back. I grew more and more irritated by the children and their irreverence for the great dead. This man was leaving letters for his heroes, little tributes to that which is eternal, and these giggling children were stealing them away like trophies? But then I rounded a corner and saw the man and the children together, poring over the scrolls. It was a game, a scavenger hunt of sorts. The kids darted so easily between the crypts. As if a grave wasn't frightening or terrible to them but rather the most natural thing in the world. Later, in front of Oscar Wilde's flying angel tomb, the man asked us for directions to Maria Callas. Of course I knew. My mother had turned to me every morning on that trip and asked, "So what will we do today?" I was the one who took responsibility for the planning, and I'd insisted we stop to buy a cemetery map.

There's this popular notion about a teen mom and her kids: *We grew up together.* That a girl who has a child will, for some indeterminate amount of time, be a sort of half-formed thing, suspended mid-metamorphosis between maiden and matron, caught between her age and her responsibility. If the baby in question is a girl, the boundary between mother and daughter will remain as permeable in life as it is in the womb. Where one leaves off and the other begins, hard to say. People will sometimes guess them to be sisters, but a sister is a separate entity, knowable and unknowable at once. The girl-mother and girl-child are more than that.

This arrangement was a central theme of the Amy Sherman-Palladino dramedy *Gilmore Girls*, which debuted on the WB soon after I graduated college. "I stopped being a child the minute the strip turned pink," Lorelei Gilmore tells her disapproving mother, Emily, to whom she has turned for help to pay for the pricey prep school her daughter, Rory, is set on attending. Lorelei ran away from the wealth and privilege of her parents' house when she had Rory at sixteen because she didn't want to be controlled. Relations have been strained, but Lorelei has put away her pride in order to help Rory "go to Harvard like she's always wanted and get the education I never got and then I can resent her for it and we can finally have a normal mother-daughter relationship!"

Throughout the pilot, it's established that Rory is "the sensible one in this house." And yet they live as "a democracy," never doing "anything unless [they] both agreed." When Lorelei does finally pull rank, she does so to keep Rory from giving up her spot at the prep school, and, by extension, the whole future she is intended to live that Lorelei didn't.

"After all, you're me," Lorelei tells her. A warning and a curse.

"I'm not you," Rory flings back at her. Is that an insult or a gift?

Lorelei and her miniature are the stars, but it's Emily Gilmore, played by the incomparable Kelly Bishop, who commands every scene she's in. My grandmother wasn't old money like the Gilmores, but she had an eye for quality and a point of view, a rococo embrace of ornamental flourishes, antique luxury, and fine fabrics, and a minor art collection that's not worth nearly as much now as her children had been led to believe it would be. She was warmer than Emily Gilmore, more effusive, likely to murmur a bawdy joke when you least expected it. If you admired a piece of jewelry or a pair of shoes she had on, she would smile coquettishly and say, "Thank you. My boyfriend gave this to me." "My boyfriend" meant the Colonel, who was smitten to the end. I didn't recognize myself in Rory Gilmore through her relationship with Lorelei. It was closer than the one I had with my mother. Too familiar, too sisterly. But I recognized the Emily Gilmore in Grandmother, who saw in me a girl she could take clothes shopping for, as she put it, a "new wardrobe to take to college in the fall," as we did over spring break my senior year in high school, when the cool girls were partying on a Panama City beach.

Back then, communal dressing rooms brought out the quick-change criminal in me, a girl who lived mostly in the margins of a notebook, in the felt-tip trail of vines snaking three-ring binder holes and spreading off rumpled corners. But in an ill-lit cavern, surrounded by adults I was sure were watching me, I was Houdini in an oversized R.E.M. T-shirt, executing a precise and complex sequence of moves to get a dress over my head without anyone seeing my meager chest and soft, untanned stomach.

I kept trying on dresses over my jeans and black chunky Mary Janes, which was one way I planned on wearing them but also a way to avoid stripping down to my underwear in what might as well have been public. This wasn't the Gap or Merry-Go-Round at the mall, where I preferred to shop, or even the K-Mart or Salvation Army thrift store, where Mom preferred the prices and thrill of the hunt, all with their individual dressing rooms where nobody could witness the awkward shame of a regular bra announcing itself outside the bounds of a strapless top.

"Let me see it without the jeans," Grandmother directed, detangling a piece of my burgundy bob from a dangling earring shaped like a daisy. "You don't wear it like that, do you?"

I stepped out of my pants and jerked out a kind of a curtsy, kicking up one foot with a mechanical flourish.

"Very chic," Grandmother nodded in approval. "Perfect for parties."

I nodded, thinking of *Animal House* and *Revenge of the Nerds*— the campus movies I'd grown up with. I couldn't picture their wild party scenes on the little liberal arts campus where I was headed.

My mother scoured the racks for hidden treasures, holding up the occasional shirt or skirt for my approval. Grandmother's mention of "a new wardrobe" sounded so extravagant, even at discount prices, and also like something out of a novel published before the moon landing. I would stroll across the campus quad in my *new wardrobe*; I would debate ethical dilemmas in my required philosophy seminar in my *new wardrobe*. I would wear this dress—a royal-blue-and-white plaid, flannel baby-doll number with an empire waist and a full skirt, an all-in-one hybrid of everything I wanted to look like that year—*to parties*, where I would only meet people with good taste in music. I stood in front of the mirror, and for the first time, I could see my new life staring back at me. For once I'd have the right clothes for it.

I slipped my jeans back on before pulling the blue dress off and reached for the next one on the pile. This one was formal, because Grandmother said I would need it, and even I could tell that the style of dresses favored by the pageant girls at my school who set the rules—dripping in beads and sequins and ersatz Southern charm—weren't going to fly outside of that small town, thank God. That dress, a black crepe halter-top column with a rhinestone collar, was more *Breakfast at Tiffany's* than Miss America. Behind me, Mom fiddled with the clasp on the collar while I tried in vain to tuck my bra straps out of sight so I could get a clearer picture in the mirror of the girl I would become in this dress, keeping my eyes trained on the top half of my reflection to ignore the puddle of jeans around my ankles.

"Exquisite," Grandmother breathed. "It's very elegant, don't you think?"

Mom finished with the clasp and beamed at me over my shoulder. I held on as long as I could before ducking away and wriggling out of the dress—anything to avoid being looked at like that. Part of me understood that all of this was supposed to have been hers first—the college visits, the scholarship essays, the date-night dresses, Grandmother shrugging off the task of choosing between two outfits with a look that said *what the hell, we'll take both*. But terrible child that I am, I didn't make myself relinquish my feeling of triumph. I had done everything that was expected of me, and therefore, I really believed that I should be allowed to have anything I wanted.

In college, I went to my first midnight showing of *The Rocky Horror Picture Show*, a rite of passage for oddball kids since 1975. But I already knew every beat of the film. I had been indoctrinated into the cult in early childhood, raised on the soundtrack. I knew the steps to the Time Warp before the Hokey Pokey, the timing of the pause in Tim Curry's pouty "antici . . . pation" as intimately as my own pulse. For my thirteenth birthday, I was finally allowed to see the film in its entirety instead of experiencing it through its musical numbers, but only from the couch in our wood-paneled family room, with a VHS tape rented from Movie Hut and my mother coaching us through the unscripted parts: *Asshole! Slut! How strange was it?! Meatloaf again!* I slipped into Magenta's seething resentment as easy as red lipstick.

The Eighth Street Playhouse in the Village, where the original Rocky Horror Official Fan Club relocated in the late 1970s after the Waverly Theater's original midnight showings closed, had been my mother's preferred venue when my brother and I were small. She started going when she was still pumping milk for me, her costume a tuxedo shirt and tails over skin-tight jeans, cowboy boots, big sunglasses, and with her long hair liberated from dozens of tiny braids into a storm cloud framing her face. She went alone. She liked the feeling of anonymity in a crowd where she felt like she belonged, of being part of something collective where nobody knew her name, let alone called her Mommy or cried to be held. Later, she told me that it felt like what she thought high school might have been like—a pep rally of sorts. Being a cradle Transylvanian, never Janet walking through the rain toward the creepy castle's light, I couldn't imagine. I remembered my own high school, its culture set by judgmental evangelical Christians. My friends and I even talking about our "Sweet Transvestite" fandom would have put the vice principal on disciplinary alert.

"Mom, high school is nothing like *Rocky Horror*," I laughed.

"Kids would probably hate it less if it were."

"How would I know?" she asked in all sincerity. "I never went."

When my mother left Fort Bragg and the Colonel's house with the award-winning garden in the spring of 1971, she didn't slip back into her prior identity as Megan Shane. Megan, the girl who had learned everything the hard way, had vanished. She became Alexis. She had turned fourteen right before leaving home, but she told everyone she was a decade older than that. She knew the ropes this time—knew how to find a place to crash, knew the places where she could work so she wouldn't have to live on panhandling. She headed straight to the Village, crashing here and there, and found her home base, Googie's on Sullivan Street across from Washington Square Park. There, the bartenders didn't care how old she looked, and the guys loved her for it. They all wanted a young girl by their side. She made friends with an artist named Kim who worked concert security, and he got her a job on his crew—the Capital Theatre, Town Hall, the waning days of the Fillmore East. She worked the Dead, Mountain, Doctors Hook and John, Hot Tuna, Procol Harum, the Beach Boys—you name the band, she kept the girls away from them, unless the band said otherwise. Some nights, she'd work the ladies' room, keeping the men out. Other nights, she'd sweep the aisles with a big flashlight, confiscating lit joints in the name of the fire department. "Sorry, guys, you know, you got to hand it over," she'd say to some kid from New Jersey. "You know, the cops are right over there watching." And into her pocket it would go with the rest until the end of the night when the crew would empty their stashes on a big table backstage and keep the party going for hours. It paid $25 a show and was a much better time than the scam she would have been running at Port Authority, soliciting donations for NORML and pocketing the cash.

She tried straight work, too, as straight as she could manage with no ID. She once walked into a boutique in the West Village owned by two guys, let's call them Seb and David, where they sold beads and baubles and hippie clothes. She had heard they hired girls to work under the table, and they paid weekly. There was another girl working there, Judy—tall with straight dark hair and kind eyes. The owners always talked about sleeping with her, loud enough for Alexis to hear. *Yuck*, she thought, and she kept her distance. But one night after work, as she cut through Washington Square Park on her way to the apartment where she'd been crashing, she saw Judy sitting on a bench. It was late, and Judy was alone.

"What are you doing out here?" Alexis asked her.

"I don't have any place to go right now," Judy said.

Alexis had somewhere to go that night, but she remembered every night when she hadn't.

"Come with me," Alexis said, and together they set off across the park. "Are you really sleeping with Seb and David?"

"No! Are you serious?" Judy said. "They told me they were sleeping with *you*."

When they got inside the building, Alexis told Judy to sit down and pretend to be asleep. Then, she ran into her friend's apartment and said, "You gotta come, there's a girl and she's passed out on the stairs." He swept her up and took her inside, then Alexis pulled Judy into the bedroom, said "I'll take care of her," and shut the door. They stayed there for a few days—maybe a week or more—and when Judy found an apartment on East Thirteenth Street and Avenue A, Alexis went with her. It was a fourth-floor walk-up, barely furnished with a mattress in the bedroom, a mattress in the living room, and a table and two chairs in the kitchen. But it was safe, and it was theirs. Someone had built a freestanding cabinet in the kitchen enclosing the bathtub, and Alexis loved to linger in the water inside that little sanctuary. One day, Judy decided they needed an exposed brick wall, so she took a hammer to the plaster herself. They had to sweep the walls for days to get rid of the loose mortar, and the room was freezing for lack of insulation, but it did look pretty cool.

The West Village, where Alexis preferred to hang out, was calmer than the East Village, but of course the rents weren't as cheap. She remembers the ghost of the grisly 1967 Groovy Murders—as the crime was sensationalized by the press—still hanging over Alphabet City at the time. Probably because one of the victims, Linda Fitzpatrick, had turned out to be a wealthy eighteen-year-old from Greenwich, Connecticut, who had attended a tony boarding school outside of Baltimore. As summer break came to an end before her senior year, she took a day trip into the city and told her parents she wanted to try to make it as an artist in New York instead of returning to school that September. "We bought her almost an entire new wardrobe," her mother told the *Times*, "And Linda even agreed to get her hair cut." Linda told Dorothy and Irving she'd be moving to the Village, letting them believe that meant Washington Square, 2 Fifth Avenue, New York University, "those dear little shops" they'd frequent on trips into the city. "But for 18-year-old Linda—at least in the last 10 weeks of her life—the Village was a different scene whose ingredients included crash pads, acid trips, freaking out, psychedelic art, witches and warlocks," the *Times* wrote in its posthumous profile. Linda was found in a basement boiler room on Avenue B, naked and bludgeoned to death with a brick, along with her friend, James "Groovy" Hutchinson, an ebullient, well-liked hippie ("an urban Huck Finn," *Esquire* dubbed him) who had once run a crash pad on East Eleventh Street that had been a frequent target of the cops and an object of fascination for the press. All any group of vulnerable kids has is each other, and all too often that isn't enough.

Alexis felt safe in her apartment with Judy, but even as she was drawn to the scene at St. Mark's Place—a poem she wrote in 1971 counted drug deals; "teenybopper runaways," which surely meant some other girls; and "the old drunk crying" among the sights and sounds—if she was being honest, her favorite part of living in the East Village was leaving for the West.

One day, passing through St. Mark's, she stepped out of Gem Spa, the newspaper stand and corner store with the good egg creams, and froze. A man wearing a brown leather bomber jacket got out of a car on the corner of Avenue A. The back of his jacket was decorated with a skull with dice for eyes and the name of her father's old Airborne company. She couldn't see the man's face to know if he was old enough to have served under her father in France or Germany, or if one of her father's men had passed the jacket down to his son or what. She felt herself wanting to run up to him and ask if he knew her father, to tell him who she really was. But she held herself back. She couldn't risk it. Who knew what kind of face he would have if he turned around?

The last time something similar like that had happened in the city, she was walking through the Village and heard someone call out to her. She almost came apart when she saw two girls from one of her old schools. They heard she had run away from home, and they were looking for her. They wanted to try a little freedom themselves.

"I cannot take care of you," she hissed to them, stuffing her hands in her pockets. It had been a rough day. "I can hardly take care of myself. If you're here, you're on your own."

A while later, she heard one of the girls had gotten involved with the Children of God. Alexis knew they targeted runaways with a seductive pitch about belonging and communal living. She'd been handed one of their palm-sized pamphlets illustrated with young freaks, *Zap Comix*-style, bearing an alluring message to lost kids seeking a collective, something bigger than themselves.

When you opened the pamphlet, there was a phone directory inside, with numbers (and in some instances, street addresses) for communes all over the US, plus several in Europe, Canada, and Mexico. There was one near New York City. Founded as Teens for Christ in 1968 by David Berg, a charismatic minister with a history of sexual misconduct, the group, also known as the Family International, reported in November 1971 that it had two thousand members in thirty-nine communes across seven countries. At that point, parent groups had already started organizing in California and Texas, where the bulk of the group's membership had been concentrated, to try to free their sons and daughters from the authoritarian sect's extreme control. Only much later would the public learn of its widespread practice of sexual, physical, and mental abuse.

What Alexis knew about it at the time was that "communal living" under strict religious rules sounded, at best, like a euphemism for controlled labor for girls—panhandling under the guise of evangelism plus domestic work at the commune. And she had heard things, like girls being used as sexual bait for recruiting men. She took one of the credit card numbers she kept for long-distance emergencies, got her old classmate's mother's number from an operator, and then said to the woman, without telling her who she was, "Look, something has to be done. Your daughter's been picked up by these people. She's going to have a life of servitude if you don't do something." The mother just freaked out. Why were adults so useless? Alexis breathed in deep, put aside all her fear and disdain, and dialed the New York State Police and told them a girl she knew had been kidnapped and that they could probably find her at this nearby commune. Maybe "kidnapped" was an exaggeration; maybe calling the cops was a betrayal. But she felt it was necessary. That girl, she thought, had no business being out on her own.

"Hey, have the guys at the store paid you yet?" Alexis asked Judy one night as they walked to Googie's for drinks. Negative. They were being stiffed, and every dollar counted. They downed more drinks and got madder and madder at the guys who had talked trash about them to keep them from becoming friends. After a few rounds, they marched down the street and barged into the store, ready to demand their cash.

"Where are Seb and David?" Alexis asked yet another girl who worked there who had probably been told they were both sleeping with the owners, too.

"They're not here," she shrugged.

Alexis and Judy got to work, flipping through the racks of dresses and blouses, grabbing anything that caught their eye: a long sequin-spangled twirly frock, a scarf shot through with silver thread, necklaces with Nepalese bell pendants that tinkled in Alexis's hands. They whirled through the small boutique, filling their arms with merchandise, and when they couldn't hold any more, they ran for the door.

"Hey, what are you doing?" the other girl called.

"Tell Seb and David to take it out of our pay!" they cried, the door banging behind them. They never went back.

Judy was a few years older than Alexis. She was also a single mom. At first, her toddler son would spend weekdays on Long Island with Judy's mother and weekends in Alphabet City with them, but once he started preschool, the schedule reversed, and Alexis would walk him to and from preschool and take care of him while Judy waitressed. They were a little family, the three of them. They'd take him to Long Island on the train on Friday after school, be young and single and free all weekend, then go back and pick him up Sunday night. The legs of the trip without him, they hitchhiked. One Sunday, they were thumbs out, headed to Judy's mother's house, when it started to rain. And even though Alexis had memorized the rules of hitchhiking, had the perils of breaking them seared into her brain, they were tired, wet, and worn down. And so, when a two-door car pulled up, with two guys who seemed local, maybe in their twenties, sitting in the front seats, Judy hopped in the back. Alexis did the only thing she could do and followed her. And now, trapped, they had to hope they would get to where they were going. Judy sat back to rest, but Alexis leaned forward. The guys were murmuring. They were talking about what they planned on doing with these two girls they had just picked up. Alexis elbowed Judy awake, and she looked out the window with a start.

"Hey, where are you going? This isn't the way," she said.

"Just sit back and relax," the driver said. "It's fine."

Alexis took her knife, the one she had bought after the terror in the motel, out of her boot and stuck it in the side of the neck of the guy in the passenger seat. Not hard. Just enough to let him know what she had. He froze.

"You need to stop the car," he told his friend. "She's going to cut me."

But his friend kept driving. Alexis looked at Judy with a tight shrug. Judy looked at her, grabbed the knife, and slid it along the side of the driver's neck, just a bit. But harder. Enough to draw blood to the surface of his skin.

"You can stop the car now," Judy said as he yelped.

Alexis finally retired the knife. Not when she moved in with my father to their apartment on East Seventh Street between Avenue B and Avenue C but when she got a dog. The legendary Duke: a black Great Dane with a white blaze on his chest, uncut floppy ears and tail, and the best manners of any canine companion, ever. This girl she knew from around but didn't like came into possession of this purebred Great Dane puppy and bragged around the building that she was going to sell it. Instead, my mother grabbed the puppy and said, "No you're not," and slammed the door in the girl's face. As Duke got bigger, you could see this gangly teenage Great Dane pulling this gangly teenage girl all around Alphabet City. Really, he walked her.

One day she was playing with Duke in the Tompkins Square Park dog run when a guy walked toward her, pointing.

"That's my dog!" he yelled.

She didn't know what to do, so she grabbed Duke's leash and ran him all the way back to the apartment, the man chasing them down Avenue B, still yelling as she and Duke ran into the vestibule of the building and locked the front door, shaken.

Two days later, she saw him again at the park and started to back away, looking for the best exit.

"Stop," he called. "I'm sorry I scared you." He jogged up to her, his hands up in peace. "Somebody stole my Great Dane and her puppies, and I thought that might be one of them. It's okay. But this dog is pulling you everywhere, isn't he?"

She nodded.

"You don't know anything about Great Danes, do you?"

She said she didn't know anything about dogs, really.

"If you don't get a Great Dane under control early, he'll never behave," the guy said. "Tell you what. If you come here to the park every day at one o'clock, I'll show you how to train him."

And with his help, she did just that. From then on, the dog went everywhere with her. Duke had so much self-control she could walk him without a leash, and he never wavered from her side. She could step inside a store, and instead of tying his leash to a parking meter, she would just tell him to sit, and he would sit by the meter and not move until she came back. With Duke, she could walk to meet my father when he got off work on Varick Street on the West Side, at two in the morning, crossing the Bowery like she owned it, and never once be bothered. "Lady, I'm just crossing the street," guys would call out to her, hands up and palms out, not wanting to be mistaken for a threat. Duke was the sweetest apartment dog—he liked to hang out the window overlooking Seventh Street, checking out the action below, his giant paws crossed in front of him like a nosy old lady—but strangers didn't know that. One night, as the family story goes, my parents were walking home from Googie's with Duke walking in the lead, and behind them, two guys were speaking Spanish. My father turned around and spoke to them in Spanish, and they fell back. He bragged to her that the men had been strategizing about how they would rob them, but he warned them that he was "very well-armed." Were they even talking about my parents at all? My father, he lied so much. But it is true that when he turned around, the men caught a glimpse of the dog my mother had trained to never leave her side. Duke, at least, was a reliable protector.

The summer before I left for college, as we packed up the things I needed for my dorm room—the extra-long twin sheets and the jumbo bins of pretzels and the new clothes Grandmother had bought for me—my mother asked me if I needed a gun. She was serious.

"You'll be in the city," she said, even though my campus was in an expensive and historic residential neighborhood tucked behind Restaurant Row, with a few headshops and coffeeshops lending the area just enough bohemian glow to have caught my eye. I scoffed at her concern. I wasn't allowed to have overnight visitors in my dorm room. Firearms were out of the question. What did she think could happen to me there, anyway? Nothing ever had. She had made sure of that, keeping a tight watch on me throughout high school, keeping me away from the things that cultivate wildness or independence, like concerts or afterschool jobs or live showings of *Rocky Horror* in the theater. I went to school like it was my job instead, did all the things I was told to do—clubs, grades, competitions—to earn scholarships so I could go to college and start my life. When my mother dropped me off for orientation, she wanted to stay longer, even suggesting she spend the night in my dorm room. I pushed her to go home sooner. I was so ready for my life to start. Here was one thing I had done first. What did I need a weapon for? "You're me," I felt she was telling me, and the only thing I knew for sure was that I wasn't.

7
Fairytales of New York

Once upon a time there was a girl who was stubborn and curious, and who didn't obey her parents. Thus begins the Brothers Grimm fairy tale "Frau Trude." As D. L. Ashliman's snappy translation then asks, "How could anything go well with her?"

The girl is curious and wants to visit the house of the mysterious Frau Trude, where strange and wicked things are said to take place. Her parents forbid her, but she goes anyway. She encounters three men on the way in, each more destructive than the last. Then she sees Frau Trude, a witch in her true form as the devil, with a head of fire. Frau Trude transforms the girl into a block of wood and throws her on the fire, praising the glow her body creates: "It gives such bright light!"

Stories like this are meant to caution wayward girls to obey, to avoid desiring knowledge of strange and amazing things. And men, especially men, because they will ruin us. But the story also recognizes that the game, according to its own rules, is rigged against the girl from the beginning: because she was disobedient, nothing good *could* happen to her. Her parents don't run out to save her from the devil with its fiery head, nor do they outfit her with the knowledge to protect herself, because they have been told they don't have to. This bad girl's fate has already been set on course.

My mother was a strong-willed girl who was curious about the world. She decided she wanted to experience it, and according to those rules, how could anything be expected to go well with her after that? Nothing else to do with a girl like that, the world decides, but throw her on the fire and let the wicked take in her glow. This is how we fail unruly girls—even if they survive the men, they still have Frau Trude to face on the other side.

There are many ways to be a good girl, though. There is my way: avoid the dangerous men, play by the official rules. But there is also another approach: accept the lies you're told and make them yours, use them for your own purposes. You can keep putting one foot in front of the other, even after meeting the charcoal burner, the huntsman, the butcher. And you can understand what the world expects from you, you disobedient girl, and let yourself be molded into that shape. You can keep walking into the fire, again and again, until all they have of you is a pile of cold ashes.

The older I got, the less good I felt I needed to be. The first Christmas I spent away from home, the year I finished graduate school, I told myself that I wasn't running away from my family but rather performing an act of filial devotion. One of my all-time favorite bands, the Pogues, had plans to reunite—including their shambolic singer, Shane MacGowan, whose precarious attachment to the band and relative states of sobriety would make any reunion urgent, necessary—for a brief tour of Ireland and the UK in December of 2004. So, at age twenty-eight, I said to hell with a holiday at home for the first time. Here was a once in a lifetime opportunity, I thought, possibly my one and only chance to see Shane perform with the full band, to be in the same room with people who shared my fierce love of this music that otherwise didn't exist outside of the jukebox. There would be other Christmas Eves at the Colonel's, I told myself, other rounds of pigs in the blanket and bottomless highballs. And besides, I thought in a flash of romantic rationalization, Daddy would have approved.

The first time I heard the Pogues, I felt the joy of recognition and the pain of longing all at once, a bittersweet cocktail. My father would have loved this band, their Irish folk rebellion run through a punk filter with a side of sea-shanty swagger. He remained dedicated to a distorted, nostalgic idea of Ireland, though the Keanes had been in the States since the mid-nineteenth century. Daddy was the kind of guy who, though frequently un- or underemployed, would boast of sending money to the IRA, a dubious yet telling claim. I remained unnamed for three days, after a birth that almost killed me, while he fought for "a proper Irish name" for me as my mother pushed for something more exotic. This wasn't just any rock show, I told myself. The way the Pogues made me feel connected to my father gave me a sort of spiritual permission to follow my own desires.

Shane MacGowan—whose continued upright existence, as of this writing, on this mortal plane is only slightly less miraculous than Keith Richards's—is the embodied definition of the crumbling romantic, a startling yet notoriously unreliable talent, dazzling and infuriating, the bombed-out ruin of his mouth somehow the only fitting vessel for his wild voice and poetic lyrics. Hard-living and tender-hearted, Shane's exploits are as legendary as his songwriting. It's hard to find mention of one without the other. Here is a snapshot, apocryphal but plausible: Once, at a dinner party, the host's baby began crying and could not be consoled. Shane got up from the table, picked the baby up, cradled it in his arms, and sang his own song, "The Broad Majestic Shannon," a lullaby for nostalgics, a memory ballad, a song for when we see each other again. The baby was soothed. Shane settled the child down to sleep, then turned around and keeled over, having passed out himself. Shane, the elegy incarnate, every quality I imbued the ghost of my father with brought back to life.

The sea shanties I memorized as a child—*What will we do with a drunken sailor, earl-aye in the morning!*—helped form a mystique around my father as an outlaw pirate that Pogues songs channeled in my heart. What adventures must have marked him into the haunted man he became? Who could expect any man to civilize himself after all that?

Every time I visited my favorite dive bar, I would punch a four-digit number into the jukebox by heart, in his honor, then sit and wait. That jukebox was so popular you'd sometimes have to kill hours to hear your songs, ordering round after round of cheap whisky highballs. By the time I would hear Shane tear into the first verse of "Sally MacLennane," my boots would be stomping the sticky floor on their own accord. A drinking song, a farewell song, a send-you-off song, a funeral song, a tribute to my father. Every night in that bar a stand-in funeral for the real one I didn't get to attend.

According to a study in the *American Journal of Psychiatry* about pediatric bereavement—a concept that went largely unacknowledged in my family—the sudden death of a parent is one of the most stressful events a child can experience, leading to increased risk for enduring depression, post-traumatic stress disorder, and functional impairment, all of which can lead to, as the study concludes, "maladaptive coping styles." Well, guilty. *Fuck it*, I thought, *Christmas in London*, and I whipped out my credit card to buy the tickets.

In the Brothers Grimm fairy tale "The Singing Bone," a wild boar rampages through the countryside. He's a real menace, this one, tearing up everything in sight. So the king decides that whoever kills the boar gets to marry his daughter. Just go with it. Three brothers accept their mission. The innocent one kills the boar, but then his scheming brothers kill him, take credit for the dead pig, and the oldest one gets to marry the princess, *huzzah*. I mean, a feral pig died for this. Those things have tusks. But this is a fairytale, so the dead brother's bones, once discovered, sing the song of truth, exposing his wicked brothers' dual crimes of murder and lying about who killed the pig, and they are executed by decree of the king. Let that be a lesson to the pretenders: an original hero is not so easily replaced.

And what of the princess? The king's prize, the ostensible motivation for carnage, betrayal, fratricide, deception, and revenge from beyond the grave? What's next for a girl who's treated like a living trophy, then widowed so young by her father's word? Freedom? Her own spin-off series? How am I supposed to know? She's not mentioned again. Look, you want a princess, just pick another—there are dozens to choose from. The tale's closing shot lingers on the dead hero's fresh grave: true slayer of the boar, that's all we need to know. Whose bones do you think the songs will be written about, anyway?

The week of the Pogues reunion was like my own personal cover of Nina & Frederik's "Christmas Time in London Town": turns through Trafalgar Square to see the towering Norwegian spruce, buying Christmas crackers and wine glasses at Harrod's to outfit the room at my South Kensington B and B, Big Ben's bells bringing tears to my eyes. In Soho, I fought my way through the crowds at Hamley's to buy a small, metal Corgi-model Batmobile for my brother made only for the UK market; in Euston, I ate budget-friendly thali at Ravi

Shankar, a recommendation from one of my poetry mentors, after Chinatown's Warren Zevon-famous Lee Ho Fuk left me cold, too crowded for the secondhand shine it might produce.

The band had booked a three-night stand at Brixton Academy, and my husband at the time and I bought tickets for two nights—insurance against Shane showing up utterly incapacitated for or ghosting at least one set. It wasn't an unfounded worry, but it was unfulfilled; Shane remained not only upright through the two-and-a-half-hour set each night, but he turned in a performance worthy of crossing the Atlantic. When we saw the band again in Chicago a couple of years later, during the death rattles of my marriage, the vibe was looser, shakier. It was a wonder it didn't careen off the rails.

But back to Nina & Frederik, and to "Christmas Time in London Town," for a minute. Danish-Dutch married aristocrats who plundered Caribbean culture for a calypso sound to help their version of easy-listening folk stand out in the sixties, Frederik made the decision for both of them, after two hit albums and one of those television shows that beautiful duos could command in those days, that it was time to retire. Nina didn't agree. They eventually divorced. She went on to become known for yet another holiday song—"Do You Know How Christmas Trees Are Grown?"—from the soundtrack of the 1969 Bond film *On Her Majesty's Secret Service*. It's the franchise's sole George Lazenby vehicle, my favorite, the marriage plot one, in which Countess Tracy, played by Diana Rigg, is the wayward daughter of the Corsican mafia boss. She becomes Bond's true love and takes a bullet to the forehead for her trouble. Tracy is transformed into a footnote, a mournful memory, reduced to glancing references in later films—Sean Connery's visit to a grave in *Diamonds Are Forever*, a pained look on Timothy Dalton's face at a wedding in *License to Kill*—and replaced by an endless parade of Bond Girls. Bond is always Bond, no matter the man who plays him. Only the girls are interchangeable.

As for Frederik, he farmed and did other things before moving to the Philippines and getting involved in transporting marijuana, according to reporting from the *Sydney Morning Herald*, for an Australian drug trafficking syndicate. Around the time I was finishing high school, Frederik and his partner Susannah died of gunshot wounds in what his obituary in the *Independent* described as "a mysterious professional killing." Frederik was actually the Baron van Pallandt. Born to an ambassador and a countess, at one point in time he owned Burke's Peerage, which published the books tracking the lineages of the nobility in the United Kingdom. Baron van Pallandt's life was made notorious by how it ended, a tragedy, an assassination related not to his rank but to his role in the underworld. It's not unlike something out of a Bond film. But what I am most interested in is the day he decided that Nina & Frederik would no longer perform. The strength Nina, beautiful and aristocratic in her own right and just as talented, must have had to decide she would not be silenced.

At Brixton Academy, fake Christmas trees stood sentry on stage, and when the band came on, the crowd, already reunion-drunk, went a little wild. But when Shane ambled out from the wings, cigarette in one hand and drink in the other, it was bedlam. He ripped into "Streams of Whiskey," which served as just a warm-up to "If I Should Fall from Grace with God." Shane's lyrics in the latter song, the title track off their third album, are layered and intricate. The conditional nature of his narrator's proposition is darkly ambiguous. Has he already killed for his cause? Is he making a pact with his brothers before setting out on a mission from which he might not return? Or is he merely testing the waters with a slant lie, a suggestion, the seeding of a myth? In this crowd, his narrator's barroom confession found credulous ears. A hand in front of me shot up with three fingers in the air when Shane growled that his lot was coming up a bad craps roll, a sailor's superstition. A body that finally finds its rest.

We sang every word to every song, and miracle of miracles, Shane, who meandered across the stage, was unsteady a few times but didn't falter, though he popped out for several breaks. The crowd lost its mind when Shane was on stage, but this reunion was also noteworthy because bassist Cait O'Riordan, who left the band after their second record, *Rum Sodomy & the Lash*, was back with the band for the first time. There wasn't a dry eye when the sidewoman stepped up to sing the traditional tune "A Man You Don't Meet Every Day," but the highlight of my evening was the encore, when she took the mic to duet with Shane on "Fairytale of New York."

"Fairytale of New York," released on 1988's *If I Should Fall from Grace with God*, the follow-up to *Rum Sodomy & the Lash*, is an establishment Christmas pop carol now and a hit in the UK and Ireland upon its initial release, but in the States in the aughts, it was just reemerging as a retro dark horse favorite, a Gen X holiday grumbler anthem, the collision of the ironic and sentimental, its yearning piano intro colliding with Shane's surprising opening lines, situating us with his character in the drunk tank on Christmas Eve. (Tom Waits's "Christmas Card from a Hooker in Minneapolis," which has been around longer, addresses similar themes—heroin, incarceration, lies, an indulgence in the what-might-have-been—but that one's a bitch to sing along with.) "Fairytale of New York" is meant to be a communal experience, despite, or perhaps especially because of, the melancholy back-and-forth of its dual vocals.

The irony of Shane's outsize persona and rough-hewn vocals is that had he been the one to sing "I'm a Man You Don't Meet Every Day" instead of Cait, it would have made a different song. But her unmistakable voice—an uppercut delivered through a velvet glove—

positions her version within the gender-flipped tradition of folk legend Jeannie Robertson's, one of the tune's most famous renditions. "Fill up your glasses of brandy and wine," she sings, "whatever it costs I will pay." There are layers—of wistfulness, of irony—a female voice adds when assuming the self-assured mantle of the "roving young fellow" Jock Stewart, his entreaty to "be easy and free when you're drinkin' with me" backed by his acres of land and men he commands and dog he did shoot—all of it both an invitation and a warning to the listener. Cait had the swagger for it. She had left home at sixteen and was living in London hostels when, like so many musicians before and after her, she joined a band after hanging around the right record store, looking for the right records at the right time. She learned to play bass, and it turned out she had a hell of a voice of her own. She, too, is an uncommon talent, and by her account also an outsized personality back then. "The band were always having to get me out of scraps," she recounted years later to the *Guardian*. "I'd start fights I couldn't possibly finish. They tolerated me, because most of the people in the band were the same, and—this was soon after punk rock—an obnoxious teenager who liked to get drunk and fight probably looked like a cool character."

When she left to go her own way after *Rum Sodomy & the Lash*, she said in that same interview, "I didn't regret leaving: I was always absolutely certain I was right." But the lovers' duet Shane was writing for Christmas had lost its second voice. Singer/songwriter Kirsty MacColl ended up stepping in to sing the part, and "Fairytale of New York" changed Christmas forever.

MacColl had died in a boating accident off the coast of Cozumel, a tragedy felt across the world, four years before that night in Brixton. This was a Pogues show during Christmas week, though. They couldn't not perform the song. And with all respect and fondness for Kirsty MacColl, her definitive performances of that song, and her absolute banger of a voice, Cait's performance has stayed with me in ways that have taken years to fully unpack. I heard lines differently in this pairing of personalities and their histories, especially in the lines about unrealized potential and the universe's caprice, in which the undead legend trades lines with the woman who walked away from a band on the rise. The generosity of Shane's writing is clear on this song, his partner's lines as unforgettable as the ones he keeps. The woman is being serenaded, but she gets to sing back. The song positioned them as equals, but I don't have any illusions that the world did on that tour—Shane would have been forgiven any stumble, but Cait had to deliver, and she did. During the instrumental break, the two bandmates stepped together and waltzed across the stage, Christmas trees twinkling in the background, fake snow swirling around them, sticking in their hair and to their shirts. Kirsty's "Fairytale of New York" is irreplaceable. Cait's is her own.

After the band and Shane parted ways in 1991, following a harrowing accident on tour, the Pogues soldiered on for a couple more albums, but it wasn't the same without him. If a brilliant but unpredictable front man becomes too much for his group to contain, it can have a hard time holding its center. Another bassist, the conventional wisdom goes, can always be found. At that point in my life, I held the great man theory of art as gospel, proof that wild creative men must be infinitely forgivable, mere victims of their own appetites, their charisma and talent making them always worth showing up for; only women had to live forever with the choices they made. I think about that now, as I keep trying to understand how the unknowns of my mother's life shaped me as much as the knowns. No matter how hard I try to focus on her, I keep coming back to the men—my father, her father, their various avatars, imagined and projected—who threaten to drive this story. They are not so easily edited from the lineup.

I had crossed an ocean that Christmas to be in Brixton that night because I needed to have faith in Shane. I believed that even degenerate geniuses are always worth waiting for but also that genius tends to take certain recognizable forms. And oh, the devotion to him in our howls. I remained attached to a slippery, nostalgia-tinged version of my father, parts of which had been manifested in Shane's songs, on stage, on my record player, in my own doubting heart. After, everyone wanted to know how Shane looked, how Shane sounded. But when I think back now to those nights in Brixton, what I feel luckiest for is having been in the room to see Cait back on stage with her band, a triumphant return all her own. What a fool any fan was to have skipped out on her shows. These days, Cait is still performing, sometimes with her old bandmate, Pogues cofounder Spider Stacy, and she hosts a satellite radio show I listen to on the drive home from my predawn swims—having given up my late nights at the dive bar for early bedtimes—where she imparts deep knowledge about musical catalogs and scenes between tracks. Recently, Shane published a hardcover volume of his drawings and writings, a striking artistic companion to his musical career. I don't believe in one kind of genius anymore. We are all capable of making something lasting and beautiful out of what we've survived.

Here is a different kind of resurrection song. Its name is "Fitcher's Bird." Once, there was a sorcerer named Fitcher, who would disguise himself to appear soft, wounded, in need of tender mercy. Maybe he swayed a bit with the jukebox's most melancholy numbers; maybe he cried into his bourbon when certain poems were recited or when choruses swelled. You don't know him, or maybe you do—there's at least one of him haunting every local scene. He used this charm to disarm beautiful girls, then he took them home and locked them up, where they were never seen or heard from again. Once, there was a girl who fell for it, like so many others before her. Maybe she saw her own need reflected in his and believed only she could truly understand. Maybe she thought she could heal him. He dragged her deep into the dark forest to his house, full of books she needed to read and records she needed to listen to and movies she really should have seen by now. But he can help. He can fill in the shameful gaps in her knowledge. She can have it all, he tells her, as long as she doesn't use this key to open this one door.

"I have a gift for you," he tells her, and for a second, she believes he has listened when she talked about the things she likes. But it turns out he's given her a big fat stupid egg. "I'm going out," Fitcher says. He's always going out. "Don't open that door."

Of course, she opens it. Girls are like that; they crave knowledge of their world. And in the room, she finds a basin full of other girls, all of them hacked to pieces. There's an axe (Jesus Christ!) and blood everywhere. The shock of it makes her drop the stupid egg into a pool of blood, and when she tries to dry it off to prove she's worthy of being given nice things, or an egg at least, she discovers she can't. When he comes home, he sees the blood on the egg and knows: *Chop chop, little love.* One more girl on the pile.

You think someone noticed when she disappeared, or came looking for her, or even asked a few simple questions when the screams echoed through the trees? Are you new here in this forest?

Fitcher goes back for the girl's sister. Same old routine. He's greedy; he returns for the third. This time, when he leaves for his very important whatever, the third girl sets the telltale egg aside on a soft, spotless pillow when she enters the room. Truth be told, she was tired of carrying it around like a hickey she couldn't hide. In the chamber of horrors, she finds her butchered sisters. She decides to work with what she's got. She reassembles them, limb by limb, biting off thread, squinting at the needle's eye, because they deserve to be buried as whole girls, not discarded like crime scene trash. But when she ties off the last bit of thread and stands them side by side, her sisters reanimate. A little stiff in places, sure, their smiles a bit ghoulish. But with a revenge story already aglimmer in their eyes.

The girls work up a plan. The mechanics of it are not important. What you need to know is that together, those girls fuck Fitcher all the way up. They make him pay. The two resurrected sisters head for home while the third hangs back to arrange a scene before slipping away. The second to last thing Fitcher sees on his walk home is a strange bird gliding past him, headed into the forest, away from his shelves of important male authors. Imagine the most ambitious junior pageant queen on the Mid-South circuit auditioning for a Jim Henson revue in a costume made only from what she could tear apart with her teeth. The third girl holds her breath as she passes him, the glitter and fake feathers of her disguise itching her arms. The last thing Fitcher sees before he runs into his house is a skull, dripping with jewels and flowers, a gruesome stunt bride grinning down at him from his upstairs window. He follows that mirage all the way up to his abattoir. The third girl, still in her sparkling bird costume, has returned with the villagers, who have finally heard the girls' cries. They set a fire and burn the horror house down to its studs with Fitcher inside.

Maybe you're thinking you would be the third girl in this story, the one who does everything right so Fitcher can't destroy her for reasons known only to him and his appetites. But the third girl isn't any braver than her sisters. She got lucky, that's all. The thing about luck is how it can fool a girl into thinking she's smarter than the others, that she can figure out how to be just good enough to keep herself from being chopped up and left for scrap. Maybe that makes you the skull in the window, a phantom bride in a princess dress—I don't know. Maybe you're a villager who looked the other way for so long because those girls had no business being in that house in the first place. If you're the first or second girl, the next version of this fairy tale is yours to write. But maybe you think this tale has nothing to do with you at all. Maybe you were told a story called "Fitcher's Bird" and didn't even think to ask why the guy is the one we remember to put in the title, why the bird doesn't even get a name. *Such a shame about Fitcher*, you're still sighing to yourself, *he was so charming. What a pity he burned himself down like that.* Look at that girl, though, dancing in triumph through the forest on her way to meet her sisters, lit up by the flames she's left behind. What else do you need to see her clearly?

8
If Your Mother Says She Loves You, Check It Out

A woman I worked with many years ago would disappear in the middle of the day to play piano in an otherwise empty room in the building we worked in together, where the late afternoon sun poured into the atrium through stately stained-glass windows. She owned a week's worth of librarian-chic office outfits, it seemed—a handful of wrap dresses and shirt shifts and cardigans—and a statement necklace or two she wore with flat boots, an indulgent austerity that dazzled me. Finally, someone I knew had mastered the art of curating a capsule wardrobe. She introduced the word "frenemy" into our vernacular. She refused to drive in a city that ran on cars. Her résumé said medical school, but she said she had quit after having an epiphany when she became a patient herself. What a way to nail a job interview for a creative position, right, a masterful pivot of weakness into strength? We talked for more than an hour in that group interview and didn't even feel the time.

She had a cool name, too, one we hadn't heard before. By the time I gleaned it wasn't the name on her birth certificate, or any expired ID she may have kept to buy wine, or the high school diploma that was maybe the highest degree she'd obtained, I felt like maybe I had never been off my own block, maybe I would swallow any line from anyone and ask for seconds. Let's say she introduced herself as "Sealeed"—and because she looked us directly in the eye when introducing herself, back in those days before smartphones were in every hand, we didn't realize, until the day it all came crashing down around her and us, that the actual way to pronounce the name typed on her résumé was "Kaylee." It has never been clear to me if she pronounced her chosen name uniquely on purpose—an extra sprinkle of *special*—or if she had only ever seen it on the page before adopting it as her own, as I have done myself with so many words I read before I ever heard them spoken. Maybe once she introduced her new self, said her name out loud, she had cast a spell that couldn't be undone.

I think about her every time a Summer of Scam-style article goes viral, with the inevitable documentary or scripted series that follows becoming fodder for the cultural discourse. The scam artist story is treated like the campy cousin to serious harm narratives: the murdered girl mystery, the shattering sex assault exposé, the insidious web of the cult tale. With a screen between the scammer and the audience, the grift, so plausible to the victims, is rendered pathetic; the people caught in its orbit too eager to believe, bless their foolish hearts, the obvious lies. In person, it's different. In many ways, hers was kind of a victimless scam. But that doesn't mean it didn't affect anyone beside herself.

The key to faking your identity is not found in TV shows about secret agents: blend in, say little, be a mystery. Instead, you want to stand out. Be a bit much. Have an audacious story. Present yourself like an open book while saying very little of substance. If you talk about yourself a lot, people don't ask many questions—they fill in the blanks for you, smooth out the question marks, perform small acts of reconciliation. A fake identity hinges on nailing just one thing: telling the scammed a story about themselves that they want to hear.

In our department in that building with the atrium and the piano, we were a tight group of creatives who cooked for each other, swapped overseas travel tips and vegetarian recipes. Years later, though we have all moved on to other jobs and homes and phases of life, we still get together for the occasional reunion. In the context of that building, we were the new media professionals helping to modernize a tradition-bound yet open-minded institution. It was interesting work with nice people that paid well enough, and "Kaylee" was good at it. It would have been an easy job for her to keep; easy, at least, for the woman she claimed to be.

She had sparkle, but she also had a mean streak. Maybe she was bored with how easy we were. After the first couple of honeymoon weeks, she began tearing through us like a tiny tornado, pushing for weak spots, messing with our minds, introducing friction into the team where before there had been none. And one day on a hunch, my boss walked upstairs and asked HR to look up a detail in this woman's background check. Hours later, she was gone.

The grapevine eventually activated. Based on the gossip, here is what I think she made up: Where she was from, her college, the medical school story. Her age as she relayed it in conversation. Quite possibly much of her work history, though some professional references had been confirmed. Her legal name, which as it turns out was quite ordinary. You couldn't mispronounce it if you tried.

Later, over martinis, my boss and I tried to figure out what the hell had happened. We were, we thought, bright people. In hindsight, there were inconsistencies and oddities we were perhaps too willing to wave away because Kaylee was charismatic and talented and felt like an interesting hire. An identity based on a lie sketches an outline around what the lie has replaced. People will fill that space in with fabrications of their own that often end up revealing more about themselves than the person living the fiction.

If I had thought about her capsule wardrobe in the context of the near-empty apartment she had invited us to one evening, for example, I might have asked myself if she was a minimalist by design or by necessity. If I hadn't been fresh out of graduate school, where I felt perpetually behind my peers on authors and concepts I felt I should have already known, I might have wondered about the knowledge gaps of hers that didn't add up and couldn't be explained by her being too cool to have cable. In retrospect, she was no master of disguise or deception.

"I think I believed her because I was raised to," I said, a wet cocktail napkin worried to shreds in my hand. I realized as soon as I had said this that it was true.

My boss's eyes widened. She cocked her head.

"Say more."

I fumbled for the words to articulate the wall of understanding that had just hit me.

"To look too closely at anyone's life is to break the rules."

I had never explicitly thought about my mother's story of her runaway years, lived as an adult with a made-up name, as "a fake identity story" until that night. Because I grew up having been taught implicitly that it was normal to be known by different identities to people from different stages of one's life, I had absorbed the lesson that a person should be accepted for who they said they were, that questioning that too deeply was a form of social betrayal. When people show you who they are, believe them—that's accepted wisdom now. What I saw for the first time in the wake of this chaotic work scam is that my family's narrative had conditioned me to believe what people told me they were. On some gut level, I felt it was only fair to give them that. My father's routine dishonesty—

sometimes dressed up in retrospect as *bullshitting*, sometimes not—was not a secret my mother kept from us. But I never thought of hers in the same terms.

I used to tell the rough outline of my mother's fake identity story often as a fun little anecdote, a bite of glam danger to consume secondhand. But until recently, I hadn't asked her directly to fill in all the parts of the story that had never quite added up. For starters, what was she doing between leaving home in 1970 and getting married in 1972? When I did start asking, and writing it all down, I realized I had absorbed a new lesson, not just from the scammer at the office but from my own work after I quit that job to go into journalism full-time. As the newsroom adage goes, "If your mother says she loves you, check it out." Which is to say, try to confirm even the most obvious details and see what else turns up when you show up to ask more questions.

My mother had mentioned once or twice in passing during my adolescence that she had once been arrested in Boston but had managed to escape. Naturally, I had questions. But her incomplete answers were incongruent with my teenage TV-drama understanding of cops and courts.

What were you arrested for?

Well, I didn't do it, so I didn't think I needed to stick around.

Did you just, what, make a run for it?

I just walked away.

Do you have a criminal record? Are you, like, wanted?

Haven't been back to Massachusetts to check.

Wait, so what exactly happened?

It's time for dinner, go set the table.

When there were holes in my understanding of the past, I filled in blanks with assumptions that made everything click. It's not that I wanted to be fooled; I just wanted the world to make sense because so much of it does not. Most people will go to great lengths to make stray pieces appear to fall into place. Hadn't I been doing that my entire life?

After my mother introduced me to her life as Megan, and traced Megan's movements from Kansas to Aspen to Boston to New York and back to her family, it wasn't that I didn't believe her. I was able to locate and secure an interview with one person who knew her as Megan—her friend Betsy—which confirmed Megan's presence in Aspen and her initial appearance in Boston. But aside from that, there was little evidence to substantiate her story. The boy she dated in New York wouldn't answer my messages, if the man I found online is even the same guy. Anecdotal corroboration is one thing journalists look for when trying to substantiate a source's story: Was anyone else there, and would they be willing to tell me what they saw, heard, did?

But there was another pathway, maybe, to corroborating Megan's tale, and not just in the margins of memories of people who had either long grown up or been folded into the creases themselves. I had the story of the Boston arrest. Around the same time that I submitted my request to the National Archives in New York for court records and case files related to my father, I sent a similar request to the Massachusetts Supreme Judicial Court Archives:

> *I'm seeking case file and court records, along with any*
> *information on the facility to which the defendant was*
> *remanded for:*
>
> *Megan (or Magan) Shane (this was an alias—she had no*
> *ID—suspected juvenile runaway)*
> *Criminal court (possibly juvenile)*
> *Arrested in Boston, or Cambridge, for shoplifting / petty*

larceny / theft at a grocery market
Time frame: 09/1970–12/1970
Held in Charles Street prison before trial; remanded to a youth
facility in Boston, 1970. Vanished from youth facility on same
day of arrival.

And another archivist angel found her for me.

My mother doesn't have a criminal record, but Megan Shane does. The wording in the court document is absurdly formal for being built around a barefoot willow of a girl who lied shamelessly to everyone, even to the face of her court-appointed attorney, one Thomas F. Sullivan Jr. Arrested on September 14, 1970, she pleaded not guilty to truancy but was found guilty in Boston's Municipal Court nine days later of being a runaway, in violation of Massachusetts Gen. Laws Chap. 272 Sec 53 Amend. Acts 1959, which carried a penalty of a $200 fine or six months in juvenile detention, or both.

She gave an address on Symphony Road as her residence. She changed her parents' names just enough to make them unfindable— her father's middle name, Sumner, with her own fake last name; her mother's maiden last name with a slant-rhymed first name, Lila, attached. The best lies are close to the truth. She tried to move her birthday by two days and nine years, but the court refused to buy that Megan Shane wasn't a minor. They marked her down as being born in 1953—six months away from eighteen, or just enough time to carry out her sentence (and four whole years older than she actually was at the time).

I have three pieces of paper and a scan of a docket to confirm the dates and rough outline of my mother's tale of being arrested in Boston, thanks to the head of archives who found the docket and pointed me in the right direction, and my friend Emily, who answered my call on Facebook for a Boston-local friend to make a trip to the courthouse to retrieve the full record—in the end, just three precious pieces of paper.

Every reporter knows the rush when the official records come through. You might discover a new source or a fresh detail that nobody had thought to mention. Perhaps they will just simply confirm that what someone had told you is, at least according to this documentation, true in the sense that it is backed up by a person or an institution with the authority to do so. Proof. But what I was looking for in Megan Shane's official records wasn't proof that my mother was telling me the truth. I believed her. I trusted her. What I needed from this quest for due diligence— and I realized this only once Emily had delivered the documents and I had examined every typed and handwritten word for its significance—was proof of something else: that Megan Shane was no master of disguise. My own eyes are not deceiving me when I look at photos of my mother as a teenager. She was just a kid. And nobody who didn't have some personal investment in doing so would have reasonably believed otherwise.

This is why fact-checking matters to the process of constructing a story and not just the verification of it before publication. Fact and truth aren't the same thing. But facts can build a solid structure for the truth you're trying to reconstruct for the reader.

Without records, official or personal, fact-checking a story requires a different kind of legwork. One method is to take what someone tells you and seek out a scaffolding of outside facts to support it, to make it a plausible story at least. My mother told me about her first Thanksgiving away from home, an interlude tucked between Megan's post-jailbreak mescaline heist and her arrival in New York at the beginning of Christmas season. When she heard two girls and a guy at the Cambridge house where she rented the little room making plans to hitchhike to Canada for a music festival, she pulled on her long underwear and her Frye boots, threw on a granny dress and her fringe jacket, stuffed as many of her scant possessions into her backpack as she could carry, and said, "I'm in." Montreal? Why not? And according to the fourth rule of hitchhiking, they needed her: three people are a tight squeeze and a tough sell; recruit a fourth and you can split into pairs, make better time, and meet up at rendezvous points along the way. On the first leg, she rode with one of the girls about two hours northwest of Boston to meet up with the other pair in a small Vermont town where the boy's sister lived. It was Thanksgiving, after all, and while Megan didn't feel a pang about missing a holiday when her father's seat would be empty at the table, her companions were eager for a home-cooked meal and a cozy overnight stay. The sister was cool, she had been assured, and there was plenty of room for everyone.

They met up on the edge of town and walked up to a small, white two-story house. Inside, a swell of people greeted them, maybe twenty in all, with a handful of longhaired toddlers running between the legs of adults drinking tea and wine and preparing a feast. She'd never seen a Thanksgiving like this: cushions on the floor in lieu of a formal dining room table; wooden spoons and chopsticks only, no silverware. And the meal itself was a far cry from James Beard's turkey with tarragon crumb stuffing like Grandmother might have served. Frances Moore Lappé's highly influential *Diet for a Small Planet* wouldn't be published for another year, but in Vermont, where cheap and abundant land had attracted an influx of idealistic back-to-the-landers, the young radicals who wanted to form organic co-ops and test their political and social ideals in the country were embracing vegetarian and macrobiotic diets. It would be a turkey-free Thanksgiving that year. Dishes heavy with brown rice, squash, beans, and lentils were passed from seat to seat, along with what

Megan found to be a distressing absence of normal Thanksgiving trimmings. No canned cranberry sauce with the ridges still intact, no marshmallow-studded sweet potato casserole. Just rustic fare and earnest politics. She didn't want to be home in Kansas with her mother and brothers, necessarily, but this alien meal didn't feel right either.

After as much brown rice as she could stomach, she slipped away from her floor cushion and out the front door. Nobody stopped her; after all, personal freedom was encouraged here, and worrying was a bummer, and it was assumed that a girl who acted like she could take care of herself would. On the road into town, she stuck out her thumb and waited for a car to slow down. When one did, she asked to be taken to any restaurant that was still serving. At a diner in town, she dug out her last couple of bucks and bought a turkey sandwich. She ate it slowly, savoring every bite, grateful for the freedom to decide for herself what she would eat and when and why. Then she hitched back to the house, where she crashed overnight with the other kids.

Border bound, they paired off differently the next day. The two girls missed each other and wanted to make the last leg together, so she and the boy devised a comfortable, plausible routine to sell to drivers—"This is my old lady/man"—and out went their thumbs and off they went. They were a little nervous about the cross into Canada. They had heard border agents had turned away thousands of young Americans trying to make their way to Bowmanville, about seventy miles east of Toronto, for the Strawberry Fields Festival back in August, kids who were unable to show sufficient ID and money—forty US dollars, to be exact—to satisfy the entry requirements to hear Robert Plant sing "Whole Lotta Love." And then on top of everything else, Zeppelin didn't even show. Kids said someone even drowned trying to swim his way across the St.

Lawrence River instead of crossing at the border. So she couldn't believe their luck when a family of three picked them up in a sedan. They could just blend in with the couple's little kid and pretend they were part of one big happy family. It would be smooth sailing through the checkpoint.

"And who are they?" the customs agent said, craning his neck around to look in the back seat after the driver showed his ID, introduced his wife and child, and told the agent where they were from, where they were going, and that no, they didn't have any food with them.

"Nice try, kids," the agent told them as Megan and the boy got out of the car and watched it pull through to another country. No money, no ID, no entry. "But you have to go back now."

Every border checkpoint has two sides. They went back through the American side, where young people who looked like them were not always greeted with kindness.

"You, come with me," a female agent told her. A man led the boy away to another room. The agent closed the door behind them, put Megan's backpack on a table, and opened it.

"Strip," she said.

Megan looked around and saw no way out of it. She shrugged out of her fringe jacket, kicked off her boots, crossed her hands at her hips, and pulled her granny dress over her head, then peeled her long johns off, top first and then bottoms. She crossed her arms over her chest, shivering in the chilly room and watching the agent toss all her belongings onto the table, flip through her books, and rifle through her clothes, looking for drugs or weapons or anything they could use to justify detaining her longer.

She had nothing.

The agent eyed her coldly.

"Okay, get out," she said.

"Just get out?" Megan echoed, incredulously, through chattering teeth. The agent walked out, letting the door bang behind her. Megan wasted no time pulling on her clothes, boots, and jacket and stuffing her things back into her bag. She needed to hurry before the agent changed her mind and returned.

The boy was waiting outside. They trudged down the road until they were out of sight of the customs checkpoint. Thumbs out, old man/lady routine in place, they waited in the cold, trying not to think of the girls who they were sure had been allowed through and were now headed to Montreal and who knows what wild and glorious adventure after that. A middle-aged man driving a semitruck pulled over and waved them in.

"Only one of you can sit up front with me," the driver said as the boy opened the passenger door and pulled himself into the cab. "It's for safety. Can't be crowded. Other one's gotta go in the bunk in the back."

"I'll go in the back," Megan said quickly, before the boy could offer up the window seat. She didn't really want to have to make conversation with the driver. After the encounter at the checkpoint, she didn't have the energy to deal with rule number three, which is to say, the lies she would hear and would have to tell herself. She figured with the boy up front, she could break hitchhiking rule number two and close her eyes for a bit. The rumble of the engine and the hum of the road lulled her to sleep.

When she woke, she could hear the boy and the driver talking. She moved to part the curtain between her and the cab, but the man's tone reminded her of something very specific and very out of place. It sounded like her mother talking to the owner of a piece of antique furniture, trying to strike a deal.

"How about I give you fifty bucks and you get out at the next gas station, just you," the driver said.

Then what? What about her? Her heart pounded. She leaned forward. She realized that she was trapped between them and the sleeper bunk.

"No way, man," the boy said, and he laughed as if to assure the driver they could both pretend this was just a dumb joke, a little bit of ribbing to pass the time on the road.

"Seventy-five."

Behind the curtain, Megan held her breath.

"She's my old lady, you know, we've been together for three years now. You know, I love her," the boy started talking faster. "She and I, we've got a good thing going. And a five-month-old baby at her mother's house we're trying to get home to now. I think we're maybe even going to get married at Christmas. Neither of us is really into that but, you know, we have the kid now, we think maybe it would be better for him, and her parents really want us to, you know. Mine too, I guess."

He was rambling, riffing, trying to build a fantasy home for her, this kid she had just met, that would convince the driver that she was permanent, a real person with people who would miss her, not a trinket to be traded by the side of the road. The trucker was trying to buy her, she realized; the boy, thank god, was buying time.

She clambered into the front seat and huddled against the boy.

"We should probably get out here if we're going to make it home, babe," she said, and they didn't breathe easily again until they had both hopped out and put all four feet on the ground. They waited until the semi disappeared into the horizon, then just a minute longer to be on the safe side, and then stuck their thumbs back out.

So here's what I'm stuck on: I can't find a record of a music festival in Montreal the week of Thanksgiving in 1970 big enough to attract the attention of a group of kids in Boston. And would I? As Megan's chattering teeth reminded me, it is cold in late November the further north one goes. It's not outdoor music festival season, at least. But that didn't stop me from burning hours chasing down rabbit holes, looking for dates and venues, trying to work backward from possible headliners and undercards. I found news stories about the Strawberry Fields debacle, but the dates didn't line up with the timing and geography of the rest of the story, with Vermont and its vegetarian Thanksgiving.

Why did it matter so much to me to find external evidence corroborating the story that happened around the conversation with the truck driver? I'm reminded, as I have been so many times while trying to fact-check my mother's memories, which range from the sharpest recollections to vague impressions, of teaching poetry students about the difference between fact and truth. The fact is my mother might have been headed to Montreal for a wild goose chase. The fact is gossip can be vague. The fact is my mother might have gone at some other time, and two stories got laid on top of each other and compressed into one. The fact is it doesn't matter because she didn't even make it across the border. The truth is she learned yet another lesson about how the cops would treat girls like her. The truth is she overheard a man trying to buy her and realized the only thing that saved her was a lucky break with a teenage boy she barely knew. Violence, grace, twisted into a cord.

I let myself go down the rabbit hole on the details of the aborted trip to Canada because I thought if I could pinpoint the public moment the story was situated inside, that would make the private exchange inside the truck—the details of which my mother remembers so clearly, decades later, though not the boy's name nor where I might find him in order to secure corroboration from an objective party, which is to say a man, that skeptical readers will demand—more believable. What we're fighting against when a woman tells her story is the immediate invalidation of her truth, despite all the statistics we have on abuse and harassment and assault: *She's lying. She wants to hurt him. He's actually the victim. She wasn't saying no then. She just wants attention.*

A fact is, as soon as my mother got back from that trip, she left Cambridge for New York, where worse things waited for her, a threat she didn't see coming. A fact is, I have disguised the identities of several men to protect their privacy. Maybe I should have worked harder to get them on record. But their stories are not, nor will they ever be, central to the truth of hers.

9
Greetings from Tatooine, Arizona

When Luke Skywalker storms away from his aunt and uncle's table after being told he has to stick around to work on their moisture farm for yet another year, he bounds up onto the flat dust, kicking rocks, silently cursing his sand-bound life. Against a bruised sky, he drinks in the setting of Tatooine's twin suns—*red at night, sailor's delight*—and sees nothing but desert wasteland. He doesn't belong here, and his blood knows it. *He has too much of his father in him*, the forlorn trumpet of John Williams's score keens. An arid breeze ruffles the rippled dunes of his hair. So swell the strings in reply: *That's what I'm afraid of.*

At age seven, my big brother, John, was obsessed with *Star Wars*, so of course I was too. He led me through the movie's best parts, jumping from scene to scene using the action figures from our pockets, while we waited at an airport gate. We were being flown to the desert, where our mother was waiting for us. I was five years old. In the Denver airport, a snowstorm raged around us—a "layover," a word we had just learned, on Hoth we decided, slicing invisible tauntaun bellies open to shelter us from the cold—while our mother's brother ferried us to our destination. *What's the cargo? Only passengers . . . and no questions asked.* This must have been some kind of diplomatic mission, or maybe reconnaissance, to be smuggled on board with only a distress call programmed inside me. Surely, we'd be back on our home planet soon. I didn't know then that Alderaan could really be blown to bits like that.

Grandmother and the Colonel had retired from Washington, DC, to a sleek ranch house in a town called Yuma in the Arizona part of the Sonora desert, on the Colorado River across from Southern California, where the late-November warmth felt dangerously foreign to us.

Yuma's landscape was alien to my eyes. I knew the controlled chaos of city streets and the pristine waterfalls and pines of the Poconos, but not this: palm trees and cacti, dusty rock everywhere, the constant rainbowing whoosh of sprinklers across manicured lawns. Orange trees just grew in people's yards. Any time you wanted to scoop one up and eat it you could. The trees were painted white up to the point where the branches shaded the trunk, to better deflect the damaging ultraviolet rays. In the desert, even trees got sunburns. I was scolded for peeling flakes of white off the bark of the orange tree in the front yard. It was so tempting, though, to worry my little fingernail under an exposed flap of latex, to see how long and uninterrupted a curl I could cultivate if I was patient and diligent and attracted no attention. If I was focused, I believed, I could skin a tree alive.

My brother and I hadn't made friends in Arizona yet, but we only needed two to play *Star Wars* if we doubled up on parts. I was the girl, so I was supposed to play Leia. But I was not a princess. Her wild-eyed defiance, her steely reserve, her quick thinking, even her regal white robes—I couldn't fit into any of that. John was the oldest so he played Han Solo, the cocky pilot who could make the Kessel Run in twelve parsecs. He wasn't born knowing how to outdraw a bounty hunter, but who is? In this new world of year-round short sleeves and cowboy boots, surrounded by strange music and stranger accents, we were immediately marked. The playground might as well have been the cantina, full of aliens eyeing us like we were the droids they didn't serve around here. The Colonel told John how to stop it:

punch just one kid right in the nose. *The blood will scare them off.* One day in the neighborhood, a circle of kids surrounded John, and one boy stepped up. *He doesn't like you. I don't like you either!* The Colonel drove by and slowed his white Caddy landcruiser to a crawl. Instead of intervening, he barked an officer's order out of his window: "Punch him in the nose, John!" He drove away, chuckling. John curled his fingers into a fist, took a swing, and blackened the kid's eye instead, and a whole diplomatic mission had to be deployed. And me? *This little one's not worth the effort.*

Another act of violence had set all this in motion—the move, the heat that can't only come from one sun—which I didn't know until much later, when I was almost an adult and needed to learn that men aren't fixed like a mountain but packed like sand, able to shift suddenly with the weather.

My father hit my mother. Frightened men do that. She had taken a punch before. One day, she stood up to her full height, hit him back, and told him if it happened again, she would leave. She knew how to make herself disappear. He knew that about her by then. John and I became the anchors. It took another eight years for her to have to make good on her promise. It started again when she went back to school, got her nursing license, built a profession. Some part of him, it would seem, couldn't stand it, that this girl might not need him anymore.

One explanation my mother gives for why she married a man twenty years older than her in the first place, when she was just a girl with nothing but open doors ahead of her, is this: she felt older than her fifteen years when they met, and he, then thirty-six and only clean for a couple of years, had lost about a decade to heroin addiction. So emotionally, they basically met each other in the middle. Really, when you think about it, they were kind of the same age.

But nothing she tells me about their marriage sounds like a match of equals. Like the time she overheard Daddy saying—between

Budweiser sips, as a family friend flipped burgers on his suburban backyard grill—that once Mom finished nursing school, he'd never have to work again. How he controlled all their money, even after she graduated and started working as an LPN, even when he wasn't working at all. One time, when he gave her $20 to go to the store for groceries and she lost it, he berated her for weeks about her stupidity and how she couldn't be trusted. When she found the bill later, folded up small in her jeans pocket, she gave it back to him. I want to climb into another science fictional universe in order to time travel back to that moment and yank it out of her hand before she can offer it as proof that she is not what he says she is.

Now, reading the letters he wrote to her after she left him, he sounds more paternal to her than partner, which is both ludicrous and entirely understandable; I can detect hints of their marriage's dark side in the patronizing way he encourages her attempts to break away and build a new life. I know what a controlling, contemptuous, fearful man sounds like. He sounds more fatherly when addressing her than he does to us. His pride in her independence is double-edged; he also wants to use it to shame her into compliance. He has no idea who he's talking to. I can see this now.

"Blame it all on Adam & Eve," he waxes philosophical to her in one letter, writing himself into an epic role. Blame for anyone but himself. "Alone is lousy," he writes also, and "nothing is irrevocable except death," which was coming, though he didn't know that yet. It was early into their separation, and he was still trying to convince her to come back; it was tucked between his claim that he was one of the few who *really* loved her and his insistence that John and I not be more disrupted than we already were. He didn't know that a wildlife specialist had brought lizards to our new school, that I had seen a Gila monster up close, sluggish but full of deadly venom, and that I'd learned the horned lizard, if provoked, could shoot blood out of its eyes. He didn't know that after, I had stalked a slinky silver-green lizard up against the fence near the swimming pool and caught it in my hand. Would its bite kill me fast or would I waste away slow? Would its bloody venom blind me? It jackknifed its sleek body and leapt out of my grasp, scurrying off into the landscaping. Between my thumb and forefinger, I pinched a twitching tail that ended abruptly in mid-air. I dropped it like a lit match.

Some of his letters are startling in how they shift back and forth between adult subjects—his advice on our housing as he's still working out his own, the details of how the recession is affecting the job market, and his tapering off the "program" (methadone)—and the rumbling about Santa Claus that adults default to in December when they don't know what else to say to kids. It's an alcoholic's long ramble. The excerpts Mom read to us at the time were just the fun parts, though, and I thought about how I could try to be more like him, a person who knew things about movies and TV shows and could tell people what was good and what wasn't worth their time.

———————

About twenty miles outside of Yuma, across the Colorado River in California, hidden in the Buttercup Valley, are these epic sand dunes that ripple and fold like the leathery skin of a sleeping monster. In the spring of 1982, when my father, writing to us from a VA hospital in New Jersey, began to die, the Lucasfilm crew for *Return of the Jedi* started building a 30,000-square-foot sand barge in the desert. It was to be the largest location set in movie history, and it was riddled with snakes. A million dollars alone was spent clearing all the vegetation from the surrounding area to make a thriving desert ecosystem look like the wastelands of Tatooine, which drove the four different kinds of rattlesnake that lived in the area to find shade elsewhere, meaning the various production shelters and outbuildings around the set. George Lucas arrived on April 9, and the mixed American and British crew took over the Stardust Motel in Yuma. They were there to recreate Tatooine—shot originally for *Star Wars* in Tunisia—for what was, for a long time, the final Star Wars movie. They built the Great Pit of Carkoon, home of the terrifying sarlacc monster. Inside the sarlacc's maw ringed with ragged razor teeth lurked an animatronic, radio-controlled arm that nobody knew would even make it into the movie. One lifelike tentacle alone cost $50,000.

Return of the Jedi is where Luke finally becomes a man. It's where Princess Leia, as Jabba's prisoner, is collared in her metal bikini and her impeccable lip gloss. Every time she pulls away from him, he yanks her back by her chain. There are photos of Carrie Fisher sunbathing in her slave outfit next to her stand-in. If Mom had been seven or eight inches shorter, she could have laid out right alongside them; she had the look. Tatooine is where Han is dragged by Boba Fett the bounty hunter at the end of *The Empire Strikes Back*, to pay back his debt to Jabba. Luke has to return to Tatooine to rescue him, while facing the betrayal of losing his hand to the evil Lord Vader, who has revealed a dark secret: that he's the father Luke idolized, the one whose spirit he followed off this desert planet in the first place.

Across the river in Arizona, there are species of plants that don't even grow on the California side, but on film, it's easy enough to let the upper Sonoran melt into the Tunisia of your memory. It's all a galaxy far, far away—George Lucas knew that.

Back at our house, the phone rang, and it was my aunt, saying, "He's worse. I think you need to come home." We didn't know how many stuntmen were breaking bones in the sarlacc pit during the shoot. They leapt in, one by one, each confident that they would be the one to walk out, each landing in a heap at the bottom. When Daddy died, Grandmother didn't wait for Mom to come home from

New Jersey to tell us. The sooner we knew, the sooner we could adjust to life cut in half. It was out of the question to take us back home to attend the funeral. A funeral was as fantastical as the Great Pit of Carkoon. We might as well have been in Tunisia. We might as well have been on one of Tatooine's three moons.

Mom found a job as a nurse on the nearby Cocopah Reservation. We moved out of Grandmother and the Colonel's house into a tiny rental of our own. Mom slept on the couch, and John and I shared a bunk bed in the single bedroom. In Jersey City, Mom had called the bedroom John and I shared in our modest two-bedroom apartment "the nursery," like the Darling children had in *Peter Pan*. But in Yuma, that fantasy didn't work. You couldn't leave the windows open for fairies in this heat, and certainly not on the ground floor. The small slab of concrete making up our front porch swarmed with black widows, so we used the back door instead. The problem with the back door was going through the backyard, which was patrolled by the landlord's aggressive guard goose. It was a full-time job just staying alive in the desert.

When Mom fell in love with the man who is now my stepfather, we moved again, this time into a three-bedroom ranch rental of our own. In the new neighborhood, our after-school babysitter had a VCR, and our friend Stevie's dad made a bootleg copy of *Star Wars*, so all of us kids gathered in the babysitter's den to watch it every single afternoon. When we weren't watching *Star Wars,* we were acting it out, and we could do that because we had memorized every scene, every word. John was Han; he never shot first. I still couldn't be Leia. She was too good, too clever, too brave. I never knew the right thing to say at the right time. We watched *Star Wars* for the hundredth time, the trumpets heralding the opening crawl: *It is a period of civil war.* I mouthed along to Leia telling Vader, "I'd recognize your foul stench anywhere," reveling in secondhand courage. It's all I had because I was really Luke, resentful on Tatooine, whining about what I didn't have, yearning for a father I couldn't know, living for any scrap of proof that he was once alive and loved me, and finding only a dotted line I couldn't quite fill in with the stories people were willing to tell me. Did I have too much of him in me? Is that what they were afraid of? Sometimes I got tired of remembering all of the right words in the right order. There was a pit of Carkoon growing inside me and I didn't even know it, a monster taking root, growing fat on everything I pushed down into its fanged mouth. Some days it was a relief to just give in and play Chewbacca. Tilting my head back, I roared and roared and roared.

One more letter survived that year. My aunts found it for me on a recent visit to their house in New Jersey. Daddy wrote this one to his in-laws, to plead his case like they were judges who might grant some leniency in his sentence, but he must have never mailed it. I don't know if he realized he had written things he shouldn't send, or if he just forgot that he'd written it altogether. His drinking, which had already been heavy, likely escalated after we left. There were other drugs, too, though I don't know if he went back to heroin in the end. When he died in the VA Hospital, the attending doctor told Mom, who had flown back after the phone call, that the cause of death was alcoholism. She gathered all of the professional authority her nursing license gave her and told him to look again at the chart, at the stomach bleeding that had actually put my father in the hospital, at the gastritis he had developed during his time in the Marines.

Didn't that make this a service-related death? She mentioned his two kids and what the VA would pay survivor's benefits for and what it wouldn't. She looked him in the eye. Then she planned a funeral, hired a bagpiper to play "Amazing Grace," appealed to his old union to help pay for it, did one last turn through New Jersey as a widow, and flew back to the desert so her sequel could start.

He probably wasn't sober when he wrote this letter, with its litany of resentments and half-truths attempting to burnish his faults to a shine. But I think it is the most honest account of who he was when she left him, and maybe even who he was to her all along. He bemoans being depressed, unemployed, and "emasculated at home," but "at least the children's lives were stable." He catalogs how Mom's work often left him in the caretaker role with us, seething with resentment over the pride she took in her talent for nursing, how she was recognized for it, first in school and then at the hospital. "It was apparent that the children and especially unemployed me were the only obstacles," he writes, as if she were out partying instead of working in a hospital and raising two little kids. Then, the confession: "We argue. We bicker. We wound with words. I hate me. She hates she. We say worse things to each other. She says something—I can't answer—I smack / slap—I quit. No defense now. Ultimate wrong. I'm beat."

This is how I know the initial *Star Wars* trilogy is Luke's story and not Leia's: George Lucas must have realized Episode VI couldn't be called *Revenge of the Jedi* as he had originally planned because that would violate the spirit of the Force, which is to say it would not be right for Luke not to forgive his father in the end, when Vader draws his final breath as frail Anakin, no longer a dark lord but a ruined man, dying so his child can live. It would not square with the trilogy's theology if Vader's death were punishment rather than redemption. In this universe, one act of tenderness can be enough to redeem the worst of a man's sins. *Star Wars* tells us to forgive our fathers so we don't become them. But Leia didn't seem to need that lesson. She was born too strong to be tempted, or else learned too much about men in her young life to buy anything Vader might try to sell her. Luke, though, I think he understands me. The same weakness in both of us must have cracked open while we baked under those Tatooine suns.

10
The Tower

The first time I almost died I had just been born, the umbilical cord wrapped so tight around my neck it had to be unwound three times before I could find my scream. They didn't know if I would live, let alone speak, read, tie my own shoes. How often has my mother told me that story, told me how lucky I had been not to be damaged by the lack of air in my lungs? Almost undone by my own hunger. My hair came in a shock of white that matched my overexposed skin—little haunted thing, ghost girl who almost vanished before she arrived. I used my first teeth to latch tight to her, pulling her close, her howl startling me into a smile, which she took personally. She smacked the sole of my little foot as a reflex, she was that shaken, and when I kept doing it—the pain of our connection—she weaned me early to the bottle. I learned to cry to my father for sweets, growing round as a dumpling, my swaggering daddy swooping in, soothing cries with his cookie-jar hand until the doctor looked at my thigh rolls and started me on a diet. They told me saltine crackers were cookies until I believed it. You could feed me any line after that.

I almost died a second time before I turned one, when our family's apartment building caught fire. This was the second fire; the first one, sparked by a faulty TV, drove my mother, father, and brother out of their building in the East Village. It rendered an already rundown apartment uninhabitable. They had to leave the city after that. A building across the street from my father's family in Jersey City had a vacancy, and they moved there, where I was born. One morning, while my mother walked my brother to preschool a few blocks away, another fire—not in our unit, but above—caused a chunk of ceiling plaster to crash into the bassinet where I had been sleeping mere seconds before my father, hearing the commotion from above, swept me into his arms and ran.

Every death survived reorders your universe. Maybe it's your body shutting down before it finds a way back to itself, leaving a crack in your belief in the competency of your own senses that you compensate for the rest of your life. Or maybe it's your sense of safety extinguished, leaving you exposed, scrambling to assemble a new shell as fast as you can will one to grow. And maybe it's the truth that gets swept away like a broken vase, and soon enough, your eye just gets used to seeing whatever's been put in its spot on the shelf. And sometimes it's a lie that dies of exposure, replaced by a bright, painful light.

On a trip to visit my brother and his family as they prepared for his third child to be born, my mother gave me an overdue Christmas present. She hadn't wanted to trust a piece of family jewelry—a pendant that had belonged to Grandmother, an opal, which is also my birthstone—to the postal service, so she packed it along to hand down to me in person. Nestled in the box next to it was a set of tarot cards wrapped in a worn silk scarf, cream colored with a blue, green, and rust abstract expressionist design.

"This is my deck that I've had since I was a girl in New York," she said, unwinding the scarf, a gift from my father's coworker, who had brought it back for her from a trip home to India. "I want you to have it now."

I've never seen my mother read cards. It was Grandmother who played fortune-teller in our family. She always claimed to be a little psychic; another sparkling trait, in addition to her elegance, that made her uncommon among the grandmothers I knew, eccentric in a glamorous, bespoke caftan kind of way. If you lost something—a ring, say—you could call her and she would ask a few questions about it, try to get an image of what you sought in her head, get you talking about your day, and then interrupt, as if hit by a bolt of lightning, with a decisive command that would lead you to what you had lost: *Look inside the laundry hamper. Your coat pocket. Next to the kitchen sink. It never left the house with you this morning.* Her powers were limited to objects, things that would stay put where you left them. Using her psychic sight to find her missing daughter, or to see what lay ahead of that girl on the road, was not in the cards.

I'm only just beginning to open myself to such rituals and connections. I tend to gravitate to things I can see and touch and verify, preferring to adorn myself with family jewelry for protection, conducting healing rites with monogrammed teaspoons and china saucers over crystals and other New Age accoutrements. But I've been learning to appreciate tarot because I can read the cards like lines from a poem, consider the metaphor of each character in the Major and Minor Arcana in its place in the spread and the resonance I feel from it. I am learning to lean on my intuition. My mother believes in using old things, not just keeping them, so down to me she passed her deck. Handling my mother's cards is one more way I can summon the girl she was when she acquired them. The ruffling of the cardstock as it slips through my fingers in a shuffle; the careful drawing of one, two, three cards, flipping them over slowly in a line to read into the images representing our past, present, future.

Even if you don't know much about tarot, you probably recognize the look of my mother's cards. Referred to for over a century as the Rider-Waite deck, its iconic designs are based on the concepts of a scholarly mystic named Arthur Edward Waite and released commercially by the Rider Company in 1909. It's considered the modern mother deck from which thousands of variations have sprung. Only recently has it become common to refer to it as the Rider-Waite-Colman deck, which includes the name of the English artist and occultist, Pamela Colman Smith, who created the illustrations. Pamela's identity was complex. Raised partly in Jamaica, it's thought she may have been biracial. She never married or had children but rather lived with a close woman friend for decades. She lived her life finding ways to thrive in a male-dominated culture, forging ties to artists, suffragists, and notable personalities such as W. B. Yeats, Bram Stoker, the actress Ellen Terry, and Georgia O'Keeffe. For nearly a century, acknowledgment of her contribution to tarot was largely erased from the public record. Other people had to push on her behalf for her to receive the recognition she had rightfully earned. I'm never surprised when I learn of fascinating women diminished, main characters relegated to the sidelines, but I am still disappointed. Even today, we have to fight against the impulse to credit the nearest man for the work.

In all the tarot decks I've handled, the card I'm most drawn to is the Tower. Colman's illustration depicts a tall structure split by a bolt of lightning that has set it ablaze. Two figures fall from its flaming windows. I love drawing the Tower in a spread. Some think it's a negative card because it signals crisis, danger, destruction. But I have come to embrace the possibilities in seeing a demolition through to the other side. There is so much—beliefs, practices, institutions, stories that no longer serve us—that deserves to be burned to the ground. Sometimes a bolt of lightning is the fastest way to get it done.

"That is the nature of the Tower," writes Matt Stansberry in *Rust Belt Arcana*, the companion text to the first deck I ever bought myself. "One minute you are snug in some structure that you've built to avoid the chaos of life, the next you are flying out of a window and your whole damn worldview has been exploded."

In his version of the card, illustrated by David Wilson, the Tower is depicted as a downtown skyscraper. Migratory birds, dazzled by the light reflecting off the building's glass facade, lie stunned, or perhaps dead, on the ground. That was me, in the hotel room in New York thinking about *Manhattan* and Woody Allen and seeing the similarities between the movie and my family's story, me flipping through the pages of my father's federal court transcripts, me hearing Megan Shane's name for the first time, me every time I interrogated the myths I was raised on and found them to be mirages, thunderstruck each time new facts collided with my threadbare truths.

A couple of months after my mother gave me her deck, I asked her if she still felt okay about me writing this book.

"Will it hurt anyone?" she asked.

I explained that I had not named anyone accused of any harm who is still alive, with the exception of celebrities about whom I was breaking no news. And why is this the first question women are taught, in so many unspoken ways, to ask? Why aren't we more worried about losing the stories of generations of women, especially the unruly ones, than we are about upsetting others?

But I was dodging her question, wasn't I? The truth is, I hope it will hurt. As I write this, a rock star recently accused of intimate partner violence against several women, including one of his partners when she was still a teenager, was nominated for a major industry award. When women pointed to this as evidence that entertainment executives do not actually cancel the careers of men who still make them money, the defensive demands began: *How long must his fans suffer by not celebrating his art because of stories about his off-stage actions, which may or may not be true?* The implication is that having to interrupt our own pleasure to treat a woman as fully human is an irritating inconvenience. The belief that women lie about the violence done to them—for attention or revenge or just innate malice—is still very strong. We have not yet fully reached *a different time* when it comes to that.

What I also hear in those complaints is a desire to avoid the pain that comes whenever we empathize with the less powerful. It seems as though many would rather adopt an unofficial policy of amnesty for past misconducts, leaving the past untroubled and keeping the towering monuments we've built to these men intact. Running into a wall of doubt about how the world should work and who is valued in it hurts; we go to such great lengths to avoid it. After all, once you start tearing your own house down, you might not want to stop. You might realize, as I did, that you'll need to destroy a version of yourself in the process.

The day John Lennon was murdered, my family as I knew it began to die too. My father probably didn't realize it that December day Mom left him in charge of us kids and took the train into the city to gather with other mourners in Central Park, but in less than a year, she would put almost an entire country between herself and him. We would go with her, and he would die soon after. Her copy of *Double Fantasy*, the album Lennon and Yoko Ono made together and released right before Lennon's death, came with us too.

When I think about the soundtrack to my childhood, half of the songs on *Double Fantasy* make the cut. Even though the album was deliberately sequenced to alternate between John's tracks and Yoko's to reinforce its intent as a kind of dialogue, I skipped Yoko's songs whenever possible. They were too difficult and too weird, while John's were familiar and melodic. Songs like "Cleanup Time" or "Watching the Wheels" were natural accompaniments for chore time or the bus ride to school, and the soothing chimes that led into the sweetness of "(Just Like) Starting Over" were simply easier for me to love.

I didn't know Yoko's songs were the ones critics praised at the time as being cooler, more avant-garde. What I knew was that my mother kept the newspapers and magazines covering Lennon's murder and memorializing his genius, along with a cassette she'd taped off a radio station's memorial marathon. It remained tucked inside my great-grandmother's hope chest with other treasured relics for decades. I knew "Beautiful Boy (Darling Boy)" made me ache in ways that I didn't know how to name. I yearned for this album's devoted husband and father as I understood him, a hero who was safe to adore. It was an easy feeling to carry until I got a little older and felt the unjust sting of "*Yoko*" as a poisonous epithet directed at any girl whose presence changes the narrative in a way the boys don't like. I saw not only the misogyny but the racism in white men's reactions to her, too. But relitigating Beatles history was not destined to be my life's work, and I eventually moved on to my own unruly, complicated musical loves.

Then, one day, while I was browsing in a used record store, I found a copy of *Double Fantasy* on CD and, in a fit of nostalgia, bought it and popped it in for a long drive. This time, I let the whole album ride, and to my surprise, I found myself more drawn to Yoko's songs than John's. Her eerie "Beautiful Boys" felt truer to my experience of childhood than John's lovely croon. I relished the warped, winking hilarity of "Yes, I'm Your Angel," and when "Hard Times Are Over" closed out the album, with the sun pouring through the windshield as I sped down the freeway, I sang along at the top of my lungs. After, I felt exhilarated, and also a bit dumb and ashamed for having missed out on such a crucial voice when it had been right under my nose the whole time. It hadn't escaped my notice that not once during the thousands of hours I had logged listening to boys, and later men, educate me about "good music" had any of them told me I should give that album, and Yoko's tracks specifically, another listen.

Today, you can find playlists online that excise all Yoko's songs from *Double Fantasy*, replacing them with other tracks from John or even with Paul McCartney tunes. They're presumably crafted by adults who believe erasing her makes for a better album, one focused—they outright say or otherwise imply—on the true artist in the room. As cultural erasures go, a *Single Fantasy* remix is a silly and pointless gesture. Yoko's genius and influence are not going anywhere, and she even reissued *Double Fantasy* with a stripped-down remastered version that showcases the original mix, giving both their voices an even sharper release. But playlists like these are just another example of fans wanting to preserve an uncomplicated idea of an admired man, the childish impulse to skip the tracks that don't easily harmonize.

It is hard for me to separate my own youthful aversion to how Yoko's songs complicated what was otherwise a John Lennon album I loved from the implicit and explicit messages I was absorbing that told me Yoko was a selfish woman who put her own ego above great men's great art. When people would bring up Lennon's imperfect history, his faults would be contextualized as the negligible flaws of an artistic genius. There was nothing, I learned passively and early on, that Yoko might achieve as an artist that could warrant her such widespread acceptance. I might have learned to love Yoko's music earlier if I had been encouraged, even a fraction of the times I had Beatles fandom pressed onto me, to give her a chance. I might have been less susceptible to the notion that genius only takes certain forms and must be protected no matter what. Silencing is not always a reaction to speaking up about violence or misconduct. Sometimes, all a woman has to do to threaten an important man's legacy is insist, even with his full endorsement, that her voice take up the same amount of room as his. Now those *Single Fantasy* remixes just feel to me like more small points on a long continuum charting the ways we've found to dismiss stories we don't want to hear.

I'm not trying to win an argument here. Disliking Yoko Ono's music doesn't necessarily make anyone a misogynist. (Or a child.) Like all things, it's a matter of taste. But our tastes are shaped by the world around us and the messages we receive from it. Woody Allen's *Manhattan* wasn't the first story I loved that focused on an older man who's enthralled by a younger girl. First, there was L. M. Montgomery's *Emily of New Moon*, her goth alternative to *Anne of Green Gables*, in which the thirtysomething Dean Priest declares his romantic interest in Emily, a brooding orphan and budding poet, and his late best friend's twelve-year-old daughter. "I think I'll wait for you," he tells her the first time they meet. She longs to be taken seriously as a writer and a person, and Dean pays her that kind of attention. In a later book, after a near-miss engagement, Montgomery writes Emily out of Dean's plans for good, but it was decades before I found my way back to the series to read how it ends. At twelve—just about the same age and temperament as Emily—what I knew was that after Dean saves Emily's life, he tells her, "Since I saved it, it's mine."

Soon after that I watched the 1989 Jerry Lee Lewis biopic *Great Balls of Fire!*, starring a devilishly handsome Dennis Quaid as the 1950s rock star. The raucous, stylish movie directed by Jim McBride made Jerry Lee's tempestuous marriage to his thirteen-year-old cousin Myra—played by Winona Ryder, the girl I most wanted to be in the world at that time—look scandalously romantic to my own adolescent eyes. As a young adult, I got really into Ted Demme's *Beautiful Girls*, a sort of Gen X version of *The Big Chill* written by Scott Rosenberg, in which a disappointed pianist played by Timothy Hutton returns to his hometown and deals with the melancholy of facing thirty by crushing on a verbally dexterous "old soul" thirteen-year-old (Natalie Portman) who lives next door to his childhood home. ("No wonder," Janet Maslin wrote for the *New York Times* in her review, "this Lolita has the film's archest dialogue.") In the 1990s girl-power version of that old story, the script has the girl asking the man to wait for *her*.

The real-life story Myra Lewis Williams outlines in her two memoirs (the first of which *Great Balls of Fire!* was loosely adapted from) is not a schoolgirl fantasy come true, though. She had been raped by a neighbor when she was twelve (she told no one, but worried afterward about "what man would want her in such sad shape") before being whisked into her marriage to Jerry Lee, who often "made life pure hell" at home once the honeymoon wore off. Natalie Portman, in a 2020 interview reflecting on her early career roles like *Beautiful Girls*, said she knew she was "being sexualized as a child" actor and being portrayed "as this Lolita figure" in the press and that she consciously cultivated a serious, conservative image in response "to make [her] feel safe." It was her attempt to control and counteract how she was being seen. What I find especially frustrating is how much more interesting and important I find these women's real stories to be—how painfully relatable they are—than what I now recognize as the eroticized sentimentality men had written them into and crafted around them on screen.

But Hollywood was just making the stories it knew would sell. After all, how many times had I sought out the tales of my father's exploits but never my mother's daring? Her time on the road as a girl should have been a legendary tale of survival in my family, but instead, the details were kept secret, like a private, contagious shame. For half a century, my mother's story has been stuffed into the margins, while my father's secrets—how often he tried and failed to get clean, how often he ran away from accountability, how many second chances he was given, his many shameless lies, and his final, unsent confession— were kept for him. I accepted this narrative without question for so long because it rhymed with the rules of the art that was so important to me—whose films were significant, whose books were universal instead of niche, whose albums set the standards for what's good, who gets to be the story's default hero. Smashing all of that to pieces felt like letting my father die a second time. Honoring my mother's survival, moving the girl she once was around like a paper doll on a hand-drawn map to reconstruct her time on the road, is what made the heartbreak worth it.

Here is an image of my mother that I love. She's standing in front of a U-Haul packed floor to ceiling with her records, books, dresses, artwork, her starched nurse's cap, our toys for when we join her, and even some baby things she can't bear to part with. She is beaming with excitement about the possibilities ahead. It is every graduation and yearbook photo of mine rolled into one. Taken about ten years after the previous time she'd left home, she is crossing the country again, leaving my father and the city where they met and the memories it will keep for her, returning to her given name, ready to answer to it again on her own terms. She fought so hard to be free. And on the third and final time she launched herself from the flaming window of a burning tower, she made the rules of the road: she chose the vehicle, her companion, where they stopped, and the route they took. This time, she was driving.

Notes

SHE'S A BRIGHT GIRL

See the 2007 critical outcry: "AFI 100 List Takes 'Manhattan.' And Shoves It." Logan Hill, Bilge Ebiri, *Vulture*, June 22, 2007.

Dylan refused to stay silent: Dylan Farrow, "An Open Letter from Dylan Farrow," *New York Times*, February 1, 2014.

"a pariah": Wallace Shawn, "Wallace Shawn: Why I'm Still Willing to Work with Woody Allen (Guest Blog)," *The Wrap*, November 10, 2021.

the original Captain's Table: Gael Greene, "Eat, Drink, and Be Wary," *New York Magazine*, August 11, 1980.

NYPD's recently formed Runaway Unit: Ted Morgan, "Little Ladies of the Night," *New York Times*, November 16, 1975.

disappearances initially written off: Skip Hollandsworth, "The Lost Boys," *Texas Monthly*, April 2011.

the Runaway Youth Act being passed in 1974: Herbert Wilton Beaser, JD, *The Legal Status of Runaway Children, Final Report, April, 1975*, US Department of Health, Education, and Welfare, Office of Human Development, Office of Youth Development.

Fox News had published an excerpt: Julie Miller, "Mariel Hemingway Says Woody Allen Tried to Seduce Her When She Was a Teenager," *Vanity Fair*, March 25, 2015.

he showed up at her home: Mariel Hemingway, *Out Came the Sun: Overcoming the Legacy of Mental Illness, Addiction, and Suicide in My Family* (Regan Arts, 2015).

her first kiss with him on camera: Interview with Mariel Hemingway, "Mariel Hemingway—'Manhattan' The Birth of a Legend," *The New Cinema Magazine*, April 21, 2010.

breezy story previewing an orchestra's: Erin Keane, "Gershwin Expert Kevin Cole Plays with Louisville Orchestra on 'Rhapsody in Blue,'" WFPL, October 24, 2013.

"If I am confessing fully": Erin Keane, "Why Mariel Hemingway's New Revelation about Woody Allen Matters," *Salon*, March 26, 2015.

Except *Manhattan*: Woody Allen, director. *Manhattan*, United Artists, 1979.

"Woody Allen's usual genius": Claire Dederer, "What Do We Do with the Art of Monstrous Men?" *The Paris Review*, 2017.

"tries to give voice to female desire": Joanna E. Rapf, "'It's Complicated, Really': Women in the Films of Woody Allen," *A Companion to Woody Allen*, edited by Peter J. Bailey and Sam B. Girgus. John Wiley & Sons, 2013, pp. 257–276.

"Mr. Allen encouraged this confusion": Caryn James, "And Here We Thought We Knew Him," *New York Times*, September 6, 1992.

"real life that hammered that lesson home": Maureen Dowd, "Liberties; Leech Women in Love!" *New York Times*, May 19, 1999.

it is Woody Allen's "personal imperfection" that "makes him more human and real": Sam B. Girgus, "Introduction to the Second Edition—The Prisoner of Aura: The Lost World of Woody Allen," *The Films of Woody Allen* (Second Edition), Cambridge University Press, 2002, p. 5.

"meaningless, and not funny": Joan Didion, "Letter from 'Manhattan,'" *New York Review of Books*, August 16, 1979.

I wrote about the complexities of acknowledging it: Erin Keane, "The Dark Side of David Bowie: As the Mourning Goes On, We Can't Ignore His History with Underaged Groupies in '70s," *Salon*, January 13, 2016.

rounds two: Erin Keane, "What I Talk about When I Talk about Woody Allen," *Salon*, December 18, 2018.

a former model alleged: Gary Baum, "Woody Allen's Secret Teen Lover Speaks: Sex, Power and a Conflicted Muse Who Inspired 'Manhattan,'" *Hollywood Reporter*, December 17, 2018.

again when he and Soon-Yi agreed: Erin Keane, "Soon-Yi Previn and Woody Allen's Strange Charm Offensive: An Enigma Wrapped in Scandal," *Salon*, September 17, 2018.

a rare and bizarre magazine profile: Daphne Merkin, "Introducing Soon-Yi Previn," *Vulture/New York Magazine*, September 16, 2018.

"Most chilling of all": Caryn James, "And Here We Thought We Knew Him," *New York Times*, September 6, 1992.

"Tracy exists for Isaac": Joanna E. Rapf, "'It's Complicated, Really': Women in the Films of Woody Allen," *A Companion to Woody Allen*, edited by Peter J. Bailey and Sam B. Girgus. John Wiley & Sons, 2013, pp. 257–276.

"It's a remake I'd like to see": Gary Baum, "Woody Allen's Secret Teen Lover Speaks: Sex, Power and a Conflicted Muse Who Inspired 'Manhattan,'" *Hollywood Reporter*, December 18, 2018.

EARL-AYE IN THE MORNING

I looked at a printout of my father's case file: *The United States vs. Theodore Palumbo and Charles Keane*, United States District Court, Southern District Court of New York, case files retrieved from the National Archives.

how the city mobilized a mass vaccination effort: John Florio and Ouisie Shapiro, "How New York City Vaccinated 6 Million People in Less Than a Month," *New York Times*, December 18, 2020.

Founded as a working farm in 1935: Nancy D. Campbell,
J. P. Olsen, Luke Walden, *The Narcotic Farm: The Rise and
Fall of America's First Prison for Drug Addicts*, 2nd ed., South
Limestone Books/University of Kentucky Press, 2021, 12.

"The Lexington Cure": Rebecca Gayle Howell, "The Lexington
Cure," *Oxford American*, November 21, 2017.

The Narco Farm also housed the Addiction Research Center:
Campbell, Olsen, Walden, *The Narcotic Farm*, 163–190.

sung with gusto in the original shanty: "What Do We Do with
a Drunken Sailor?" Trad. (The Irish Rovers have a fantastic
recording.)

JERSEY GIRLS

Her name was New Jersey Skeleton 1972: Christine Chapman,
America's Runaways. William Morrow and Company, 1976,
269–271.

I emailed the collection manager of archaeology and ethnology:
Email correspondence with Dr. David Rosenthal, Dr. Dave
Hunt, and Dr. Doug Ubelaker, Smithsonian Institute
Department of Anthropology, November 11–27, 2018.

the stuff of Springsteen songs: Bruce Springsteen, "4th of July,
Asbury Park (Sandy)," track #2, *The Wild, the Innocent, & the
E-Street Shuffle*, Columbia Records, 1973.

Etan Patz's disappearance: Rick Rojas, "What Happened to
Etan Patz? Unraveling a Nearly 40-Year-Old Case," *New York
Times*, January 30, 2017.

"one of the thousands of restless youngsters": Tom Buckley,
"Little Girl's Search Led to Death; Deborah Neill Went from
Ohio Hamlet to Morgue Here; Lure of Hippie Life Proved Too
Much for 13-Year-Old," *New York Times*, August 12, 1968.

"who came to New York seeking adventure": Martin Arnold, "13 Accused Here of Torturing Girls to Force Them into Prostitution Ring," *New York Times*, April 6, 1971.

The year after little Beth disappeared: Veronica Fulton, "Fifty-Four Years Later, Family Demands Answers in Baby Sister's Disappearance," *Dateline*, NBCNews.com, June 14, 2019.

A medicolegal death investigator emailed me back: Email correspondence with Stacey A. Toto, Southern Regional Medical Examiner's Office, Office of the Chief State Medical Examiner, New Jersey, September 16, 2020.

the protagonist attempts to explain: Bruce Springsteen, "Atlantic City," track #2, *Nebraska*, Columbia Records, 1982.

THE RULES OF HITCHHIKING

"Teenagers are an abstraction": Christine Chapman, *America's Runaways*. William Morrow and Company, 1976, pp. 269–271.

had only finished paving its downtown streets seven years earlier: Aspen Historical Society, "The Skiing Boom: 1961–1983," aspenhistory.org.

more than 26,000 skiers per hour in peak season: Tim Cooney, "The Complete Guide to Aspen's Storied Ski History," *Aspen Sojourner*, 2015.

A sign on Main Street: Katie Redding, "Aspen Thumbing Station is Back," *Aspen Times*, January 6, 2009.

a copy of an anthology: Glenn Leggett, editor. *Twelve Poets*, Holt, Rinehart and Winston, 1961.

wasn't the only young girl: Interview with Betsy Rosenwald, September 2, 2018.

faculty of that time period: Jacob Proctor, "Avant-Garde Aspen," *Aspen Sojourner*, 2013.

It was estimated there were anywhere from: Robert Reinhold, "New Campus Problem: Young Drifters," *New York Times*, November 10, 1970.

"forged from the improbable ingredients of idealism and alienation": Jon Nordheimer, "A New Spirit Afoot in the Haight," *New York Times*, August 10, 1972.

A group of nuns drove a van: "Mission and History," Bridge Over Troubled Waters website, www.bridgeotw.org.

"both confused and confusing": Herbert Wilton Beaser, JD, *The Legal Status of Runaway Children, Final Report, April, 1975*, US Department of Health, Education, and Welfare, Office of Human Development, Office of Youth Development.

peak in 1971 at more than 200,000 arrests: Anne B. Moses, "The Runaway Youth Act: Paradoxes of Reform." *Social Service Review* 52, no. 2 (1978): 227–43.

Megan was arrested and charged: *Commonwealth of Massachusetts vs. Megan Shane*. September 15, 1970. Retrieved from the Boston Municipal Court Central Division clerk's office, November 8, 2018.

having just been murdered inside Nadja's: Arnold H. Lubasch, "2 Arraigned in Holdup Slaying of 4 Here," *New York Times*, December 2, 1970.

peaches shot through: Gael Greene, "Everything You Always Wanted to Know about Ice Cream but Were Too Fat to Ask," *New York Magazine*, August 3, 1970.

the Zap #4 obscenity trial: Joe Sergi, "Obscenity Case Files: People of New York v. Kirkpatrick (Zap Comix #4)," Comic Book Legal Defense Fund website, cbldf.org.

the formula for a DIY telephone credit card: Michael Drosnin, "Ripping Off, The New Life Style," *New York Times*, August 8, 1971.

TAKING OFF

one of his favorite Westerns: John Ford, director. *The Man Who Shot Liberty Valance*, Paramount Pictures, 1962.

In Ford's 1956 film: John Ford, director. *The Searchers*, Warner Bros., 1956.

"angrier, and more troubled than ever": Glenn Frankel, *The Searchers: The Making of an American Legend*, Bloomsbury, 2013.

the story of a real girl, Cynthia Ann Parker: Nathan Cone, "The Texas History behind John Ford's 'The Searchers,'" Texas Public Radio, April 9, 2013.

"Even as Cynthia Ann is celebrated": Jan Reid, "The Warrior's Bride," *Texas Monthly*, February 2003.

"all recent American cinema": Stuart Byron, "The Searchers: Cult Movie of the New Hollywood," *New York*, March 5, 1979, p. 45.

the greatest American western: "Welcome: AFI's 100 Years . . . 100 Movies." American Film Institute. 2008. Archived from the original on July 16, 2011. https://web.archive.org/web/20110706070516/http://www.afi.com/Docs/100Years/TOP10.pdf.

"He literally acts out the worst aspects of racism in our country": Martin Scorsese, "Martin Scorsese on Watching *The Searchers* for the First Time," American Film Institute, YouTube, posted March 13, 2013.

"Scorsese grappled with": Martin Scorsese, "Guest Reviewer: Martin Scorsese on 'The Searchers,'" *Hollywood Reporter*, March 8, 2013.

"Is the film intended to endorse their attitudes": Roger Ebert, "The Searchers," *RogerEbert.com*, November 25, 2011.

the Czech director's first American film: Milos Forman, director. *Taking Off*, Universal Pictures, 1971.

"The film's bold assertion": Steve Lippman, "The '70s Seen: Miloš Forman's *Taking Off*," *Talkhouse*, July 10, 2017.

Forman lived in and around the downtown New York scene: James Conaway, "Milos Forman's America Is Like Kafka's— Basically Comic," *New York Times*, July 11, 1971.

"What is not so well understood about Liberty Valance": David Coursen, "John Ford's Wilderness: *The Man Who Shot Liberty Valance*," *Sight and Sound*, Autumn 1978, Volume 47 No. 4, reprinted in *Parallax View*, May 21, 2009.

THE QUEEN OF ALPHABET CITY

"I stopped being a child the minute the strip turned pink": Amy Sherman-Palladino, writer; Lesli Linka Glatter, director. *Gilmore Girls*, Season 1, Episode 1, WB, first aired October 5, 2000.

timing of the pause in Tim Curry's: Jim Sharman, director. *Rocky Horror Picture Show*, 20th Century Fox, 1975.

one of the victims, Linda Fitzpatrick: J. Anthony Lukas, "The Two Worlds of Linda Fitzpatrick," *New York Times*, October 16, 1967.

"an urban Huck Finn": Anthony Lukas, "The Life and Death of a Hippie," *Esquire*, May 11, 1968.

a poem she wrote in 1971: Alexis, "St. Mark's Place," personal archives.

When you opened the pamphlet: Children of God pamphlet, personal archives.

two thousand members in thirty-nine communes: James T. Wooten, "Ill Winds Buffet Communal Sect," *New York Times*, November 29, 1971.

Only much later would the public learn: Steven Brocklehurst, "Children of God Cult Was 'Hell on Earth,'" *BBC Scotland News*, June 27, 2018.

FAIRYTALES OF NEW YORK

Once upon a time: Jacob and Wilhelm Grimm, "Frau Trude," *Grimms' Fairy Tales*, no. 43.

"How could anything go well with her?": D. L. Ashliman, "Frau Trude," Folklore and Mythology Electronic Texts. https://sites.pitt.edu/~dash/ashliman.html.

"It gives such bright light!": Ibid.

According to a study: David A. Brent, MD, Nadine Melhem, PhD, et al., "The Burden of Bereavement: Early-Onset Depression and Impairment in Youths Bereaved by Sudden Parental Death in a 7-Year Prospective Study," *American Journal of Psychiatry*, Volume 175, Issue 9, September 1, 2018, pp. 887–896.

In the Brothers Grimm fairy tale: Jacob and Wilhelm Grimm, "The Singing Bone," *Grimms' Fairy Tales*, no. 28.

my own personal cover of Nina & Frederik's: Nina & Frederik, "Christmas Time in London Town," *A Season's Greeting from Nina & Frederik*, Columbia Records, 1966.

yet another holiday song: Nina, "Do You Know How Christmas Trees Are Grown?" *On Her Majesty's Secret Service,* Original Motion Picture Soundtrack, EMI, 1969.

the marriage plot one: Peter R. Hunt, director. *On Her Majesty's Secret Service*, United Artists, 1969.

Sean Connery's visit to a grave: Guy Hamilton, director. *Diamonds Are Forever,* United Artists, 1971.

Timothy Dalton's face: John Glen, director. *License to Kill,* United Artists, 1989.

As for Frederik, he farmed: Kate McClymont, "Drug Tsar Uses Silence in Fight to Keep Villa," *Sydney Morning Herald,* December 16, 2006.

"a mysterious professional killing": Karl Dallas, "Obituary: Frederik van Pallandt," *The Independent,* May 22, 1994.

the title track off their third album: The Pogues, *If I Should Fall from Grace with God,* Universal/Island Records, January 18, 1988.

after their second record: The Pogues, *Rum Sodomy & the Lash,* Stiff/MCA, August 5, 1985.

an establishment Christmas pop carol now: The Pogues, "Fairytale of New York," track #4, *If I Should Fall from Grace with God,* Universal/Island Records, January 18, 1988.

heroin, incarceration, lies: Tom Waits, "Christmas Card from a Hooker in Minneapolis," track #3, *Blue Valentine,* Asylum Records, September 5, 1978.

one of the tune's most famous renditions: Jeannie Robertson, "I'm a Man Youse Don't Meet Every Day," track #12, *Scottish Songs and Folk Ballads,* Prestige Records, 1960.

"The band were always having to get me out of scraps": Cait O'Riordan, as told to Dave Simpson, "The ones that got away," *The Guardian,* June 1, 2009.

lost its second voice: "The Story of 'Fairytale of New York,'" documentary, BBC, directed by Carl Johnson, 2005.

a harrowing accident on tour: Dave Simpson, "Old Habits Die Hard," *The Guardian,* November 25, 2004.

a pricey hardcover volume: Mark Yarm, "Shane MacGowan Wants a Lot More of Life," *New York Times*, December 28, 2021.

Once there was a sorcerer: Jacob and Wilhelm Grimm, "Fitcher's Bird," *Grimms' Fairy Tales*, no. 46.

IF YOUR MOTHER SAYS SHE LOVES YOU, CHECK IT OUT

Strawberry Fields Festival: Ken Kelley, "The Day Led Zeppelin Was Booked to Play in Shediac, NB," *FYI Music News*, August 9, 2016; Sean Gadon, "Fifty Years Ago, Canada's Answer to Woodstock Was My Coming of Age," *Toronto Star*, July 19, 2020.

TATOOINE, ARIZONA

When Luke Skywalker storms away: George Lucas, director. *Star Wars*, Lucasfilm Ltd., 1977.

a 30,000-square-foot sand barge in the desert: J. W. Rinzler, *The Making of Return of the Jedi*, Del Rey, 2013.

where Luke finally becomes a man: Richard Marquand, director. *Return of the Jedi*, Lucasfilm Ltd, 1983.

"Blame it all on Adam & Eve": Charles "Red" Keane, letters, family archive.

THE TOWER

Pamela's identity was complex: Lakshmi Ramgopal, "Demystifying Pamela Colman Smith," *Shondaland*, July 6, 2018.

She lived her life: Sharmistha Ray, "Reviving a Forgotten Artist of the Occult," *Hyperallergic*, March 23, 2019.

"That is the nature of the Tower": Matt Stansberry, *Rust Belt Arcana*, Belt Publishing, 2018, p. 110.

the album Lennon and Yoko Ono made together: John Lennon and Yoko Ono, *Double Fantasy*, Geffen Records, November 17, 1980.

Yoko's songs were the ones critics praised: Kenneth Womack, "What Critics Got Wrong about John Lennon and Yoko Ono's 'Double Fantasy,'" *Salon*, December 12, 2020.

the album was deliberately sequenced: Geoff Edgers, "John Lennon's Most Revealing Album Was Also his Last," *Washington Post*, November 12, 2020.

"I think I'll wait for you": L. M. Montgomery, *Emily of New Moon*, Frederick A. Stokes Company, 1923.

In a later book: L. M. Montgomery, *Emily's Quest*, Frederick A. Stokes Company, 1927.

the 1989 Jerry Lee Lewis biopic: Jim McBride, director. *Great Balls of Fire!* Orion Pictures, 1989.

a sort of Gen X version of *The Big Chill*: Ted Demme, director. *Beautiful Girls*, Miramax, 1996.

"this Lolita has the film's archest dialogue": Janet Maslin, "Beautiful Girls," *New York Times*, February 9, 1996.

"what man would want her in such sad shape": Myra Lewis (with Murray Silver), *Great Balls of Fire! The Uncensored Story of Jerry Lee Lewis*, St. Martin's Press, 1982, p. 70, 256.

"being sexualized as a child": Natalie Portman interviewed by Dax Shepard, *Armchair Expert*, podcast, December 7, 2020.

Acknowledgments

Portions of this book were published first, in different form, in *Salon*. No family's story can be told in one sitting, in one voice. This one is mine. It wouldn't have been possible without the hours my mother spent on the phone, telling me stories, and her generosity in allowing me to write about her experiences in my own words. Thank you for indulging my curiosity, for being patient with me when I yelped in surprise and indignation, and for always supporting my writing. This book also would not have been possible without the support of my husband, Drew, whose boundless love and patience, not to mention his enthusiasm for movie night, made the last four years possible. Thanks also to my big brother, John, whose memory is sharper than mine and always available for backup, and to Uncle Russ and Aunties Regis and Mary Jo for your memories, photos, and documents, and for answering my intrusive questions; to Betsy Rosenwald for taking my call and trusting me with your memories; to Judy O'Brien for being such a good friend to my mother; to Emily Ruddock for taking on the Boston mission; to Martha Bayne for talking me out of a tree; and to my old crew for the reunion. My eternal gratitude to the brilliant Anne Trubek for her clear vision and unflagging enthusiasm for this book, even when I chose the more difficult option; to my insightful and careful editor, Michael Jauchen, for his rigor and understanding; and to the entire team at Belt: Phoebe Mogharei, Meredith Pangrace, William Rickman, and David Wilson. I owe so much to the wisdom and faith of Laura Morton, the only person to have read every single version of this book. If we hadn't run into each other that New Year's Eve after the year neither of us wrote and decided we would trade pages and keep each other on track, this book would not exist. Here's to our bold girls, wherever their adventures take them. I'm especially grateful to Eden Davis Stephens for her eagle eye and excellent advice. Thanks also to the generous encouragement and emotional and professional support from Sean Cannon, David Daley, Sadie Dupuis, Brigid Kaelin, Alice Martell, Melanie McFarland, Beth Newberry, Molly Peacock, Pamela Reese, Heather Schröering, Kevin Smokler, D. Watkins, Jaki Watson, Mary Elizabeth Williams, Katy Yocom, the whole team at *Salon*, my Spalding Naslund-Mann family, and my Beer Therapy and Fancycakes friends. Thank you.